THE
PUEBLO

THE
PUEBLO

Alfonso Ortiz
University of New Mexico

Frank W. Porter III
General Editor

CHELSEA HOUSE PUBLISHERS
New York   Philadelphia

On the cover   Traditional-style Pueblo pottery from San Ildefonso.

Chelsea House Publishers
Editorial Director   Richard Rennert
Executive Managing Editor   Karyn Gullen Browne
Executive Editor   Sean Dolan
Copy Chief   Robin James
Picture Editor   Adrian G. Allen
Art Director   Robert Mitchell
Manufacturing Director   Gerald Levine
Systems Manager   Lindsey Ottman
Production Coordinator   Marie Claire Cebrían-Ume

Indians of North America
Senior Editor   Sean Dolan

Staff for **THE PUEBLO**
Copy Editor   Nicole Greenblatt
Editorial Assistant   Joy Sanchez
Senior Designer   Rae Grant
Picture Researcher   Sandy Jones

3 5 7 9 8 6 4 2

Library of Congress Cataloging-in-Publication Data

Ortiz, Alfonso, 1939–
    The Pueblo / by Alfonso Ortiz.
       p.   cm.—(Indians of North America)
    Includes bibliographical references and index.
    Summary: Examines the history, culture, and traditions of the Pueblo. Includes a photo essay on their crafts.
       ISBN 1-55546-727-X.
          0-7910-0396-5 (pbk.)
    1. Pueblo Indians. [1. Pueblo Indians. 2. Indians of North America—Southwest, New.] I. Title. II. Series: Indians of North America (Chelsea House Publishers)
E99.P9077   1992   91-24888
979'.00497—dc20   CIP
                                                            AC

CONTENTS

INDIANS OF NORTH AMERICA

CHELSEA HOUSE PUBLISHERS

INDIANS OF NORTH AMERICA: CONFLICT AND SURVIVAL

Frank W. Porter III

The Indians survived our open intention of wiping them out, and since the tide turned they have even weathered our good intentions toward them, which can be much more deadly.

John Steinbeck
America and Americans

When Europeans first reached the North American continent, they found hundreds of tribes occupying a vast and rich country. The newcomers quickly recognized the wealth of natural resources. They were not, however, so quick or willing to recognize the spiritual, cultural, and intellectual riches of the people they called Indians.

The Indians of North America examines the problems that develop when people with different cultures come together. For American Indians, the consequences of their interaction with non-Indian people have been both productive and tragic. The Europeans believed they had "discovered" a "New World," but their religious bigotry, cultural bias, and materialistic world view kept them from appreciating and understanding the people who lived in it. All too often they attempted to change the way of life of the indigenous people. The Spanish conquistadores wanted the Indians as a source of labor. The Christian missionaries, many of whom were English, viewed them as potential converts. French traders and trappers used the Indians as a means to obtain pelts. As Francis Parkman, the 19th-century historian, stated, "Spanish civilization crushed the Indian; English civilization scorned and neglected him; French civilization embraced and cherished him."

7

Nearly 500 years later, many people think of American Indians as curious vestiges of a distant past, waging a futile war to survive in a Space Age society. Even today, our understanding of the history and culture of American Indians is too often derived from unsympathetic, culturally biased, and inaccurate reports. The American Indian, described and portrayed in thousands of movies, television programs, books, articles, and government studies, has either been raised to the status of the "noble savage" or disparaged as the "wild Indian" who resisted the westward expansion of the American frontier.

Where in this popular view are the real Indians, the human beings and communities whose ancestors can be traced back to ice-age hunters? Where are the creative and indomitable people whose sophisticated technologies used the natural resources to ensure their survival, whose military skill might even have prevented European settlement of North America if not for devastating epidemics and disruption of the ecology? Where are the men and women who are today diligently struggling to assert their legal rights and express once again the value of their heritage?

The various Indian tribes of North America, like people everywhere, have a history that includes population expansion, adaptation to a range of regional environments, trade across wide networks, internal strife, and warfare. This was the reality. Europeans justified their conquests, however, by creating a mythical image of the New World and its native people. In this myth, the New World was a virgin land, waiting for the Europeans. The arrival of Christopher Columbus ended a timeless primitiveness for the original inhabitants.

Also part of this myth was the debate over the origins of the American Indians. Fantastic and diverse answers were proposed by the early explorers, missionairies, and settlers. Some thought that the Indians were descended from the Ten Lost Tribes of Israel, others that they were descended from inhabitants of the lost continent of Atlantis. One writer suggested that the Indians had reached North America in another Noah's ark.

A later myth, perpetrated by many historians, focused on the relentless persecution during the past five centuries until only a scattering of these "primitive" people remained to be herded onto reservations. This view fails to chronicle the overt and covert ways in which the Indians successfully coped with the intruders.

All of these myths presented one-sided interpretations that ignored the complexity of European and American events and policies. All left serious questions unanswered. What were the origins of the American Indians? Where did they come from? How and when did they get to the New World? What was their life—their culture—really like?

In the late 1800s, anthropologists and archaeologists in the Smithsonian Institution's newly created Bureau of American Ethnology in Washington,

D.C., began to study scientifically the history and culture of the Indians of North America. They were motivated by an honest belief that the Indians were on the verge of extinction and that along with them would vanish their languages, religious beliefs, technology, myths, and legends. These men and women went out to visit, study, and record data from as many Indian communities as possible before this information was forever lost.

By this time there was a new myth in the national consciousness. American Indians existed as figures in the American past. They had performed a historical mission. They had challenged white settlers who trekked across the continent. Once conquered, however, they were supposed to accept graciously the way of life of their conquerors.

The reality again was different. American Indians resisted both actively and passively. They refused to lose their unique identity, to be assimilated into white society. Many whites viewed the Indians not only as members of a conquered nation but also as "inferior" and "unequal." The rights of the Indians could be expanded, contracted, or modified as the conquerors saw fit. In every generation, white society asked itself what to do with the American Indians. Their answers have resulted in the twists and turns of federal Indian policy.

There were two general approaches. One way was to raise the Indians to a "higher level" by "civilizing" them. Zealous missionaries considered it their Christian duty to elevate the Indian through conversion and scanty education. The other approach was to ignore the Indians until they disappeared under pressure from the ever-expanding white society. The myth of the "vanishing Indian" gave stronger support to the latter option, helping to justify the taking of the Indians' land.

Prior to the end of the 18th century, there was no national policy on Indians simply because the American nation had not yet come into existence. American Indians similarly did not possess a political or social unity with which to confront the various Europeans. They were not homogeneous. Rather, they were loosely formed bands and tribes, speaking nearly 300 languages and thousands of dialects. The collective identity felt by Indians today is a result of their common experiences of defeat and/or mistreatment at the hands of whites.

During the colonial period, the British crown did not have a coordinated policy toward the Indians of North America. Specific tribes (most notably the Iroquois and the Cherokee) became military and political pawns used by both the crown and the individual colonies. The success of the American Revolution brought no immediate change. When the United States acquired new territory from France and Mexico in the early 19th century, the federal government wanted to open this land to settlement by homesteaders. But the Indian tribes that lived on this land had signed treaties with European governments assuring their title to the land. Now the United States assumed legal responsibility for honoring these treaties.

At first, President Thomas Jefferson believed that the Louisiana Purchase contained sufficient land for both the Indians and the white population. Within a generation, though, it became clear that the Indians would not be allowed to remain. In the 1830s the federal government began to coerce the eastern tribes to sign treaties agreeing to relinquish their ancestral land and move west of the Mississippi River. Whenever these negotiations failed, President Andrew Jackson used the military to remove the Indians. The southeastern tribes, promised food and transportation during their removal to the West, were instead forced to walk the "Trail of Tears." More than 4,000 men, woman, and children died during this forced march. The "removal policy" was successful in opening the land to homesteaders, but it created enormous hardships for the Indians.

By 1871 most of the tribes in the United States had signed treaties ceding most or all of their ancestral land in exchange for reservations and welfare. The treaty terms were intended to bind both parties for all time. But in the General Allotment Act of 1887, the federal government changed its policy again. Now the goal was to make tribal members into individual landowners and farmers, encouraging their absorption into white society. This policy was advantageous to whites who were eager to acquire Indian land, but it proved disastrous for the Indians. One hundred thirty-eight million acres of reservation land were subdivided into tracts of 160, 80, or as little as 40 acres, and allotted tribe members on an individual basis. Land owned in this way was said to have "trust status" and could not be sold. But the surplus land—all Indian land not allotted to individuals—was opened (for sale) to white settlers. Ultimately, more than 90 million acres of land were taken from the Indians by legal and illegal means.

The resulting loss of land was a catastrophe for the Indians. It was necessary to make it illegal for Indians to sell their land to non-Indians. The Indian Reorganization Act of 1934 officially ended the allotment period. Tribes that voted to accept the provisions of this act were reorganized, and an effort was made to purchase land within preexisting reservations to restore an adequate land base.

Ten years later, in 1944, federal Indian policy again shifted. Now the federal government wanted to get out of the "Indian business." In 1953 an act of Congress named specific tribes whose trust status was to be ended "at the earliest possible time." This new law enabled the United States to end unilaterally, whether the Indians wished it or not, the special status that protected the land in Indian tribal reservations. In the 1950s federal Indian policy was to transfer federal responsibility and jurisdiction to state governments, encourage the physical relocation of Indian peoples from reservations to urban areas, and hasten the termination, or extinction, of tribes.

Between 1954 and 1962 Congress passed specific laws authorizing the termination of more than 100 tribal groups. The stated purpose of the termination policy was to ensure the full and complete integration of Indians into American society. However, there is a less benign way to interpret this legislation. Even as termination was being discussed in Congress, 133 separate bills were introduced to permit the transfer of trust land ownership from Indians to non-Indians.

With the Johnson administration in the 1960s the federal government began to reject termination. In the 1970s yet another Indian policy emerged. Known as "self-determination," it favored keeping the protective role of the federal government while increasing tribal participation in, and control of, important areas of local government. In 1983 President Reagan, in a policy statement on Indian affairs, restated the unique "government is government" relationship of the United States with the Indians. However, federal programs since then have moved toward transferring Indian affairs to individual states, which have long desired to gain control of Indian land and resources.

As long as American Indians retain power, land, and resources that are coveted by the states and the federal government, there will continue to be a "clash of cultures," and the issues will be contested in the courts, Congress, the White House, and even in the international human rights community. To give all Americans a greater comprehension of the issues and conflicts involving American Indians today is a major goal of this series. These issues are not easily understood, nor can these conflicts be readily resolved. The study of North American Indian history and culture is a necessary and important step toward that comprehension. All Americans must learn the history of the relations between the Indians and the federal government, recognize the unique legal status of the Indians, and understand the heritage and cultures of the Indians of North America.

An elderly Pueblo Indian man from San Juan, the largest and northernmost of the six Tewa-speaking north pueblos. San Juan is on the east bank of the Rio Grande, about five miles of the town of Española.

IN
THE
BEGINNING

In the beginning, so the story goes, the people traveled upward from their homes beneath the ground until they emerged from the underworld through a lake at the sacred place called *shipapu*, to which, after their death, they would return after a short journey and reenter the underworld.

But now the people wandered, across a great continent, through a countryside of deserts and plains and mountains, led by their chiefs, who cleared a path for them, and aided by the Great Spirit and other sacred beings, known as *kachinas*, who showed the people how to make their way in this new world. The people learned how to build, and how to plant crops, especially corn, which had been given them by a sacred being known as Iatiku, the Grandmother; and how to hunt; and how to dance in order to honor their gods, who brought them and showed them so many beautiful and valuable things.

And at this time the people were one, and they prospered. They built rooms and then houses and then entire great buildings, consisting of many rooms and homes that were connected by ladders and constructed one on top of the other, with terraces in front, from stone and dried mud. Some of these buildings had five stories and 800 rooms. Entire villages were built on the top of flat, tablelike hills known as mesas. And the sacred ones showed the people how to water their nearby fields using terraces and canals and reservoirs, and the people were not hungry, and they were many and healthy.

But there was danger in this world above as well, floods and tornadoes and drought, as well as warlike enemies, and the people moved often, looking for that

The probable ancestors of the Pueblos, the Anasazi ("ancient ones" in Navajo), built spectacular multitiered apartment buildings in the recesses of canyon walls, where they were safe from attack by their enemies.

place where they could live in peace with themselves and all that surrounded them. The sacred ones continued to help them, and they built towering dwellings along the walls of cliffs where their enemies could not reach them.

Finally, the Great Spirit told the people that they must move again, to a place that he would show them where the rain would fall in springtime and the snow in winter, where there would be no drought or floods and their enemies would not bother them. So the people moved again, south, to the beautiful country along the Rio Grande, where

their life was so harmonious and prosperous, and their numbers became so great that they began to spread out away from each other and establish many separate villages and even to speak different languages from one another. But before they did, the Great Spirit and the sacred ones reminded them of many different things that they were all to remember always if they wished to live in peace: how to plant and tend their crops; how to treat one another with dignity and respect, and how to greet strangers with hospitality; how to protect themselves from their

This young Pueblo man from Acoma, the "sky city," was photographed by Edward S. Curtis in 1904. The westernmost of the Keresan pueblos, Acoma is built on top of a 400-foot mesa some 50 miles west of Albuquerque, New Mexico.

of New Mexico. The word *pueblo* is a Spanish one, meaning "village" or "town," and was used by the first Europeans to describe these peoples because of the magnificent, year-round stone and adobe dwellings and villages in which they lived. The civilization of which these pueblos were representative was one of the oldest in North America; when the Spanish *conquistadores* arrived in the Rio Grande valley in New Mexico in the 1540s, the Pueblos had already been living in their harmonious villages for hundreds of years, and their ancestors, the Anasazis, or Ancient Ones, had built an equally impressive civilization on the mesas and cliffs of the region known today as the Four Corners, where the boundaries of Colorado, New Mexico, Arizona, and Utah intersect.

Though the Spanish—noting only the superficial similarities of the construction of their homes and villages, their skill as farmers, and their devotion to a religion seemingly centered around secret, circular underground chambers known as kivas—grouped all these village dwellers together as Pueblos, in so doing they overlooked several significant differences among them. As the historian Joe Sando, a Pueblo from Jemez, put it in *Pueblo Nations: Eight Centuries of Pueblo History*, the "pueblos share a common traditional native religion, although rituals and observances may vary; a similar lifestyle and philosophy; and a common economy based on the same geographical region occupied by them for thousands of years. But the pueblos have an independence similar

enemies, and how to extract a prosperous living from a land that some would see as barren and brutal; how to remember and obey their laws and their leaders, and how to remember their gods in prayer and ritual and dance. Above all, the Spirit instructed them to remember all that they had been through together, and that they were one people, and so would always remain.

So the American Indian peoples known collectively as the Pueblos tell the story of how they came to occupy their homeland in what is now the state

An aerial view of Acoma today. The presence of automobiles and trucks has not altered the essential character of the pueblo, which with the Hopi settlements is in all likelihood the oldest continuously inhabited village in the United States.

to that of nations; although they are in close proximity to one another, and subject to the same natural forces, each maintains a unique identity. Thus the pueblos have common elements, but are distinctive entities in their own right. The languages spoken vary greatly, even within dialects related to a single stock.''

Today, there are 19 remaining inhabited pueblos in New Mexico: Taos, Picuris, Nambe, Pojoaque, San Ildefonso, Tesuque, San Juan, Santa Clara, Jemez, Cochiti, Sandia, San Felipe, Santa Ana, Santo Domingo, Zia, Isleta, Acoma, Laguna, and Zuni. All 19 are in the northern part of the state; most are on or near the Rio Grande and its tributaries, except for Zuni, which is much farther west. These 19 Pueblos are generally grouped by scholars into three different language groups: The Tanoan (Taos, Picuris, Sandia, Isleta, San Juan, Santa Clara, San Ildefonso, Nambe, Tesuque, Pojoaque, and Jemez); the Keresan

(Acoma, Cochiti, Laguna, San Felipe, Santa Ana, Santo Domingo, and Zia); and the Zuni (Zuni). In addition, the Tanoan language group is broken down into three separate dialects: the Tiwa (Taos, Picuris, Sandia, and Isleta); the Tewa (San Juan, Santa Clara, San Ildefonso, Nambe, Tesuque, and Pojoaque); and the Towa (Jemez). Most modern inhabitants of these 19 pueblos speak English as well as their traditional tribal language; village elders may speak Spanish as well, although few members of the young generation do.

The Hopi Indians, who reside in 13 villages farther west, in Arizona, are also a Pueblo people, but for various reasons, geography not smallest among them, their history over the last four centuries has been somewhat different than the New Mexico Pueblos, and the Spanish influence on their culture has been much less pronounced. Although the Hopis will be mentioned in this volume, the primary focus will be on the New Mexico Pueblos and their success in maintaining one of the oldest cultural traditions in North America. One of the first Native American peoples to experience direct contact with whites, the Pueblos have also been one of the most successful at maintaining their traditions and identities as a people. Unlike most other Indian peoples, for example, the Pueblos still live in their traditional homeland, the one their Great Spirit helped them to find hundreds of years before the arrival of soldiers on horseback from a different world across the sea. ▲

An Acoma Pueblo child with pottery. Many of the Pueblo cultural traditions that non-Indians tried to eradicate are now a source of livelihood for the Indians.

A woman of Picuris pueblo, photographed in 1979. Twenty miles south of the city of Taos, New Mexico, Picuris is a small, Tiwa-speaking village that though continuously inhabited since at least 1591 is today home to no more than a few hundred people.

THE
MYSTERIOUS
NORTH

The reports sent to the royal courts of their mother country by the Europeans who explored the New World in the 16th century often contained a curious mixture of fact and fantasy. Lured by such chimeras as the Garden of Eden (which Christopher Columbus believed he found off the coast of Venezuela on his third voyage) and the Fountain of Youth (sought after by the Spanish conquistador Ponce de Léon), adventurers sought both riches and immortality in the newly discovered continent. Accordingly, the first Spanish attempts to explore the homelands of the Pueblo Indians, in what is now the American Southwest, were motivated by long-lived tales of the fabulous wealth of the so-called Seven Cities of the Antilles, which according to legend had been founded somewhere to the west by seven bishops fleeing the Moorish invasion of Spain in 734.

Initially, the Seven Cities were believed to lie on islands in the unex-plored ocean far to the west of Europe, until 1528, when an Indian slave in the service of the conquistador Nuno de Guzman recounted how as a boy he had traveled into the interior of the lands beyond the northern frontier of the Spanish territory in Mexico to trade feathers for silver and gold. According to Guzman's account, "Tejo had accompanied his father once or twice and said that he had seen seven towns so large that they could be compared in size to Mexico and its suburbs, and that in them were whole streets occupied by silversmiths."

In 1536 came still another report, this time to the viceroy of New Spain, Don Antonio de Mendoza, from the four lone survivors of the ill-fated Pánfilo de Narváez expedition to Florida. After being shipwrecked off the coast of what is today Texas, these men had spent the next eight years wandering among the numerous Indian groups living in the

19

region, sometimes as celebrated healers, other times as mistreated slaves. Their leader, Álvar Núñez Cabeza de Vaca, upon finally reaching Mexico City, told a tale of adventure and hardship that encouraged the proposition that the Seven Cities were in fact located in a rich northern province:

> We marched more than a hundred leagues through continuously inhabited country . . . where corn and beans remained plentiful. The people gave us innumerable deerhide and cotton blankets, the latter better than those of New Spain, beads made of coral from the south sea, fine turquoises from the north—in fact, everything they had, including a special gift to me of five emerald arrowheads such as they use in their singing and dancing. These looked quite valuable. I asked where they came from. They said from lofty mountains to the north, where there were towns of great population and great houses, and that the arrowheads had been purchased with feather bushes and parrot plumes.

By the time he reached Mexico City, Cabeza de Vaca had lost the "emerald arrowheads," which were probably malachite, and so had no direct proof of any

The improbable trek of Álvar Núñez Cabeza de Vaca and his three companions across the Southwest—"country so remote and malign, so destitute of all resource," he characterized it—from the approximate site of present-day Galveston, Texas, to the Gulf of California helped give rise to the Spanish belief in the so-called Seven Cities of Cíbola, "large and powerful villages, four and five stories high."

riches, but the party's accounts of "large and powerful villages, four and five stories high, of which they had heard a great deal" were enough to interest Mendoza in a reconnaissance trip to the North, to the region the Indians called Cíbola.

The group selected for the expedition included a Franciscan clergyman, Fray Marcos de Niza; several christianized Pima Indians; and one of the four survivors of the shipwreck, a dark-skinned Moor named Esteban, who was to serve as guide and envoy during the trip. De Niza was instructed by the viceroy to obtain all relevant information regarding the geography, topography, natural resources, and inhabitants of the northern lands; to claim the land in the name of the king of Spain; and to convert to Christianity the natives living there.

Fray Marcos's party left the northernmost Spanish frontier settlement, Culiacan, in the present-day Mexican state of Sinaloa, on March 7, 1539. Accompanied by Sobaipuri Indians, by mid-May, Esteban, who was leading an advance party well ahead of the main body of the expedition, had forged northward as far as the Zuni pueblo of Hawikuh, in west central New Mexico near its present-day border with Arizona, where he explained to the inhabitants that he had come "to establish peace and to heal them." Ignoring several warnings and indications that he was not welcome, Esteban boasted of the size and military prowess of the expedition that was following not far behind him, according to a Yuma Indian who told the tale two years later to a different group of Spanish invaders, whereupon the Zuni "killed him and tore him into many pieces . . . so that he would not reveal their location to his brothers." Thus, at their initial encounter with non-Indians, the Zunis immediately perceived the threat to their civilization posed by the invaders.

Unnerved by the news of Esteban's death, Fray Marcos, it seems most likely, immediately planted a cross, claimed the land for Spain, and, "with much more fear than food," turned back south for the long return journey to Culiacan, which he reached in June 1539. Though many would later question whether the friar laid eyes on Hawikuh at all—he said he glimpsed it at a distance from a hill—he did provide a glowing description of the pueblo, which he claimed was bigger than Mexico City. This report further excited Spanish interest in Cíbola, and Viceroy Mendoza wasted little time in publicly announcing Cíbola's discovery and plans for an expedition to conquer it.

A new Spanish force, under the command of Francisco Vásquez de Coronado, now made the long march across mountain and desert from Culiacan to Hawikuh, a trip made even more perilous by the message the Zuni had sent to some of the outlying tribes. If the Spanish passed their way, the Zuni said, "they should not respect them, but kill them, for they were mortal. They were sure of this they said, because they had the bones of the one who had gone there. If they did not dare to do it they should notify them and they would come and do it themselves."

The conquistador Francisco Vásquez de Coronado leads his entrada toward Pueblo country in this painting by 19th-century American artist Frederic Remington.

The Indians at Hawikuh had long expected the Spanish to return to avenge Esteban's murder, and they were ready for Coronado and his men when they arrived at the pueblo in early July 1540. The women and children had been evacuated to the top of a nearby mesa, and only the warriors and several older men, who served as war captains, remained to defend the village. When the Spaniards, arrayed in battle formation outside the pueblo walls, read aloud a requisition that demanded the Indians proclaim their obedience to the Christian god and the king of Spain, they received in response a shower of arrows. But the Spanish, in armor and on horseback, using their "canes that spit fire and made thunder," were a formidable enemy, and though Coronado was knocked unconscious, they succeeded in taking Hawikuh. The age-old culture of the Pueblo Indians was about to be forever changed.

With the Indians having "fled to the hills, leaving their towns deserted, with only some few remaining in them," the Spanish took time to examine their conquest. For the most part, they were disappointed in Hawikuh because it did not measure up to Fray Marcos's grandiose descriptions, and the wealth, in gold and silver, the conquistadores had expected to find in Cíbola was nowhere in evidence. "I can assure you," Coronado wrote Mendoza, "that [Fray Marcos] has not told the truth in a single thing that he said, but everything is the opposite of what he related, except the name of the cities and the large stone houses."

There were certain aspects of the Pueblo culture that did greatly impress the Spanish, however. Hungry as they were after their long campaign, in the course of which their provisions had long since run out, the Spanish marveled at the Cíbolans' agricultural prowess, noting that although the native corn did not grow tall, "each stalk bears three and four large and heavy ears with 800 grains each, a thing never seen in these regions." They were equally impressed by the Zuni's skill as architects and expressed their wonder at discovering elaborate stone and adobe structures that were seven stories high.

The Spanish also took special note of the way the pueblo was governed:

> They have no rulers as in New Spain, but are governed by the counsel of their oldest men. They have their priests, whom they call papas, who preach to them. These priests are the old men, who mount the high terrace of the pueblo in the morning as the sun rises, and from there, like town criers, preach to the people, who all listen in silence, seated along the corridors. The priests tell the people how they should live. I believe they give them some commandments to observe, because there is no drunkenness, sodomy, or human sacrifice among them, nor do they eat human flesh, or steal.

While Coronado waited for the main body of his army to join him at Hawikuh, his lieutenants were dispatched in various directions to verify reports about other provinces. The Spanish first visited the Hopi towns in northeastern Arizona, where they obtained guides who led them to, among other places, the Grand Canyon.

Word quickly spread among the various Pueblo groups "that Cíbola had been conquered by very fierce men who rode animals that ate people." Reactions to Spanish forays into the areas surrounding Hawikuh were mixed. At Hopi and Acoma, for instance, the Indians confronted the Spaniards with weapons and warned them not to cross symbolic lines they had drawn on the earth, but such resistance usually crumbled with a display of Spanish might, and more often the Indians offered the newcomers articles such as cotton cloth, animal hides, and corn as signs as peace.

Representatives of a large pueblo to the east, Cicuye (Pecos), visited Coronado at Hawikuh, extending an offer of friendship to the Spaniards. They told Coronado of huge herds of large, shaggy cattle—the buffalo, which Cabeza de Vaca had also spoken of—that roamed the prairies to the east. When Coronado sent a small reconnaissance party in this direction, he soon received word that good winter quarters had been found along a wide river that was lined with many other villages. This, of course, was the Rio Grande valley, where the majority of pueblos, then as now, were located.

Coronado moved his force east, to a province called Tiguex, where the Spanish displaced the residents of a Tiwa pueblo. Though the ongoing Spanish presence led to escalating hostility between the natives and newcomers,

The Zunis defend the pueblo of Hawikuh from Coronado and his men in July 1540. One of Coronado's soldiers, Pedro de Castaneda, was surprised to discover that the Pueblos were not savages: "There is no drunkenness among them nor sodomy nor sacrifices, neither do they eat flesh, but they are usually at work."

one Spanish soldier, Pedro de Castaneda, was able to make detailed observations of Pueblo culture. As the Spanish had been at Hawikuh, Castaneda was most impressed by Pueblo architecture and the harmonious way of life of the inhabitants of the multistoried adobe "apartment" buildings. Castaneda described the native mortar of charcoal ash and dirt and *estufas* (ceremonial chambers, known more commonly as kivas) with floors paved with large slabs like the baths of Europe, some having 12 pillars and "so large that they could be used for a game of ball." He also expressed admiration for the cleanliness of the residents and their dwellings, their "jugs of such elaborate designs and shapes," and the cooperative work habits of the people.

But the natives of Tiguex were not as docile as they seemed. In a short time they rebelled against the presence of the Spanish, who quelled the uprising with extreme brutality, burning many Indians at the stake and laying siege to two pueblos. The natives of Tiguex soon retreated to impregnable mesa tops, abandoning their 12 villages to the conquistadores.

Recognizing that the Spanish force was too strong to be defeated militarily, the Pueblos now tried cleverness. An Indian captive of the Spanish began to regale them with marvelous tales of the way of life in his native Quivira, to the east, across the vast plains, where, he claimed, "the common table service of all was generally of wrought silver," while "the pitchers, dishes, and bowls were made of gold." After a long journey eastward across the bewildering buffalo plains, Quivira was revealed to the Spanish to be nothing more than a gathering of grass huts in what is today the state of Kansas. Under torture for his deception, the mendacious guide revealed that "the people of Cicuye had asked him to take the Spaniards out there and lead them astray on the plains. Thus, through lack of provisions, their horses would die and they themselves would become so feeble that, upon their return, the people of Cicuye could kill them easily and so obtain revenge for what the Spaniards had done to them."

A disappointed Coronado returned to Pueblo country and remained there for another winter. In the almost two

The Pueblo villages have not greatly changed in the more than 450 years since the first Spanish entrada. Shown here is a photograph of Acoma taken in 1904 by Edward S. Curtis. One of Coronado's lieutenants, Hernando de Alvarado, characterized Acoma as "one of the strongest [forts] ever seen."

years that the Spaniards had spent in this region, they had visited most of the villages up and down the Rio Grande as well as to the east and west. They had come to know the extent of Pueblo country and the types of people who occupied it. But there were no riches in the sense that Coronado and his men had hoped, and they returned to Mexico in the spring of 1542 empty-handed and disillusioned. Two Franciscan friars remained behind to preach Christianity to the pueblo dwellers, but they were killed soon after the others departed. Coronado's report to the viceroy proved such a disappointment that the viceroy decreed perpetual silence about the expedition. For the time being, the mysterious north had lost its allure for the Spanish, and the Pueblo Indians were left alone to resume their centuries-old way of life. ▲

A deer dancer from San Juan pueblo. Pueblo religious life is extremely complex and is organized around membership in various societies. According to Pueblo historian Joe S. Sando, "The Pueblos have no word that translates as 'religion.' The knowledge of the spiritual life is part of the person twenty-four hours a day, every day of the year."

RESISTING
THE
INVADER

The next Spanish expedition to the mysterious north set forth on June 5, 1581, for the purpose of peacefully converting the Pueblos to Christianity. Upon reaching the Rio Grande valley, its members—9 soldiers, 19 Indian servants, and 3 Franciscan missionaries under the leadership of Fray Agustín Rodríguez—discovered that Indian memories of the Spanish remained strong; as the Spanish approached, the Pueblos systematically retreated to the mountains, where the expedition's horses could not follow.

Exploring the deserted pueblos, the Spanish were pleased to find "very well planned" houses built in blocks, with whitewashed interiors "well decorated with monsters, other animals, and human figures." In addition to great quantities of pots, jars, and pans "all decorated and of better quality than the pottery of New Spain," the Spaniards encountered several household items obviously unfamiliar to them, which they describe only as "many curious articles, more neatly wrought than those of the Mexicans [Aztecs] when they were conquered."

After sending word that he had come in peace, Rodríguez claimed that "there was not a day when we were not surrounded and accompanied by more than twelve thousand people." In the course of the several months it spent in Pueblo country, the expedition, according to its chronicler, a man named Gallegos, visited no less than 57 separate pueblos. Initially, the generosity of their inhabitants toward the newcomers was overwhelming; according to Gallegos, so great was the quantity of corn tortillas, corn-flour gruel, calabashes, and beans bestowed upon the party that it was said that each day there was enough left over to feed 500 men.

Gallegos recorded many details about the day-to-day life of the Pueblos, whose industrious and harmonious way of life greatly impressed him. The Pueblo men were generally in the fields, which were watered by means of complex systems of irrigation, tending to their crops of corn, beans, and squash, by daybreak, while the women produced pottery "so excellent and delicate" that they "equal, and even surpass, the pottery made in Portugal." Gallegos described in great detail some of the ceremonies of the ancient and complex Pueblo religion, whose secrets, then as now, the Indians were careful to guard from outsiders:

> During the month of December they begin to perform their dances. They continue more than four months at intervals of a certain number of days, every fifteen days, I believe. Attendance at the [ceremonies] is general, so the people gather in large numbers, though only the men take part, the women never. The ceremonies, which begin in the morning and last until evening, are held around an altar maintained for this purpose and continue throughout the night.

Gallegos also described in detail such other elements of the Pueblo religion as prayer sticks, the practice of whipping, and ceremonial clowns, and he provided an account of a snake dance. The Spanish took particular note also of such curiosities of Pueblo life as underground doghouses and corrals containing flocks of 100 turkeys. They were intrigued by the manner in which the women transported their family's water supply: "For

this the Indians make and place on their heads a cushion of palm leaves, similar to those used in Old Castile, on top of which they place and carry the water jar." The Spanish found "it all very interesting," but they were most impressed with the richness of the Puebloan textiles, which Gallegos described at length, marveling at the colored woven cotton cloth, the blankets "decorated with many figures and colors," the hand-painted and embroidered cotton shirts and skirts, and embroidered sashes adorned with tassels.

But relations between the Spanish and the Indians soon soured, largely because the Spanish insisted, once their own provisions were exhausted, on treating the pueblos as inexhaustible storehouses. At a pueblo the Spanish called Piedra Aita, the mounting hostility turned into fighting when the Indians refused to provide the Spanish with food. Overwhelmed by the Spanish guns, "which roared a great deal and spat fire like lightning," Gallegos recorded an Indian as saying, the Pueblos were made to give up nine loads of cornmeal to the invaders. Soon, other pueblos as well were forced to feed, supply, and house the Spanish.

For this bounty, Gallegos wrote, the Spaniards gave thanks to God and were pleased that the Pueblos were becoming accustomed to the forced tribute, as they predicted it would thereby make the Indians less resentful when permanent settlements were established. It was thus taken for granted that the tribute network that the Spanish colonists had

Acoma pueblo as photographed from the Catholic church there by Edward S. Curtis in 1904. The Spanish introduced Catholicism to the Pueblos and achieved a high rate of nominal conversion, but the true basis of most Pueblos' spiritual life remains their traditional religion.

imposed upon the indigenous population of New Spain would be extended into the northern territories.

A truer indication of Pueblo sentiment came in September, when Fray Juan de Santa María, anxious to report on what he had seen, departed alone for Mexico. According to Gallegos,

> When the natives saw that the friar was leaving, they became alarmed, believing he was going to bring more Christians in order to put them out of their homes; so they asked us by signs where he was going, all alone. We tried to dissuade them from their wicked thoughts, but, as they were Indians, this did not prevent them from doing evil. They followed the friar and killed him after two or three days of travel.

By the time the remaining members of the Spanish expedition, in January 1582, prepared to make their return to Mexico, they had "realized clearly and definitely that [the Indians] wanted to kill us, and that the people of the entire region were gathering for this purpose." Nevertheless, the three friars insisted on remaining behind to preach the gospel to the native inhabitants of the land; the clergymen were killed soon after the soldiers departed. The retreat of the remainder of the expedition was punctuated by several belligerent encounters.

After the soldiers' return to New Spain without the friars, a party, under the leadership of Don Antonio de Espejo and Fray Bernardino Beltrán, was organized for the rescue of the clergymen. Espejo reported that the Rio Grande valley was heavily populated, with more than 12,000 Indians living in their apartmentlike dwellings on either side of the river. As many scholars have pointed out, Espejo's description accurately depicts a way of life that would remain unchanged, in many of its essentials, to the early 20th century:

> As we crossed this province the inhabitants of each town came out to meet us, took us to their pueblos, and gave us quantities of turkeys, corn, beans, and tortillas, with other kinds of bread. . . . They grind raw corn on very large stones, five or six women working together in a single mill. . . . Their houses are two, three, or four stories high, each house being partitioned into a number of rooms; and in many of the houses there are estufas for the winter weather. In the pueblos each plaza has two estufas, which are houses built underground, well sheltered and tightly closed with benches inside to sit on. At the entrance to each estufa there is a ladder for going down into it, so that strangers may find shelter there, and a large stack of wood.
>
> In this province some of the natives are clad in cotton blankets, buffalo hides, or dressed chamois skins. . . . some of them wear shirts.
>
> The women have cotton skirts, often embroidered with colored thread, and over the shoulders a blanket like that worn by the Mexican Indians, fastened at the waist by a strip of embroidered material, with tassels. . . . everyone, man or woman, wears shoes or boots with soles of

buffalo hide and uppers of dressed deerskin. The women arrange their hair neatly and prettily, winding it with care around molds at each side of the head.

> All the pueblos have caciques . . . who in turn have other caciques under them, . . . the *tequitatos*, the latter functioning like sheriffs to execute the orders of their superiors. . . . When the Spaniards ask for something from the principal caciques of the pueblos, these officials summon the *tequitatos*, who then proclaim the order loud throughout the pueblo concerned and in a very short time all bring what they may have been asked to provide.
>
> In every one of these pueblos there is a house to which food is brought for the devil. The natives have small stone idols which they worship; and also, just as the Spaniards have crosses along the roads, these people set up, midway between pueblos, their artificial hillocks (cuecillos) built of stones like wayside shrines where they place painted sticks and feathers, saying that the devil will stop there to rest and talk to them. They have fields planted with corn, beans, calabashes, and tobacco (piciete) in abundance. These crops are seasonal, dependent on rainfall, or they are irrigated by means of good ditches. . . . in each planted field the worker has a shelter, supported by four pillars, where food is carried to him at noon and he spends the siesta; for usually the workers stay in their fields from morning until night.

The Indians' response to this newest Spanish *entrada* (literally meaning entrance, the term was used for the various Spanish expeditions of exploration and conquest in the American interior) ran the usual cycle of fear, hospitality, and hostility. After being lured back from the surrounding mountains by Espejo's assurances that he and his men had come in peace, the Indians overwhelmed their visitors with banquets of rabbit, venison, tortillas, *atole* (a soft drink made of maize flour), beans, calabashes, corn, and pinole. There was often music and dancing, and the Indians strewed cornmeal along the way to the pueblo of Walpai to welcome the newcomers. Their initial fear, the Indians explained, was due to their memory of the violence that Coronado had perpetrated on the various pueblos. In at least one pueblo, the explorers found evidence of the friars' presence in the form of a newly erected cross, which the Indians had allowed to remain standing but festooned with feathers and pinole.

But as the other Spaniards before them had done, Espejo's band exhausted their host's hospitality with their unending exactions of food and turquoise and demands for gold and silver, and they soon began to abuse the Indians. At a pueblo called Puaray, Espejo responded to the Indians' refusal to feed his group by imprisoning 30 of them in an estufa and burning them alive. A pueblo named Puala was set ablaze, and 16 Indian captives "were lined up against some cottonwoods close to the pueblo ... where they were garroted and shot many times until they were dead."

The Pueblos' fears about the ultimate

A snake dance at Walpi pueblo, one of the Hopi villages, in 1895. The eminent art historian Vincent Scully wrote of the ceremonial dances of the Pueblos: "The dances themselves I believe to be the most profound works of art yet produced on the American continent."

intention of the Spanish proved well founded. Despite the ultimately hostile reception he received, Espejo reported that the Rio Grande valley was a favorable spot for colonization. Accordingly, in 1590, Gaspar Costano de Sosa led an expedition of approximately 170 would-be colonists north along the Pecos River to the vicinity of the pueblo of Cicuye, where they arrived in December.

This time, the Pueblos were not willing to give the Spanish the benefit of the doubt regarding their intentions. An advance party was routed in a skirmish

A member of a Pueblo kushare *society. (*Kushare *is the Keresan word for such individuals; the word is* Kosa *in the Tewa language and* Tabosh *in Towa.) The word is usually translated into English as meaning* clown, *but the kushares served a most serious purpose in Pueblo society. Through the use of ridicule and buffoonery, according to the historian Henry Warner Bowden, they shamed "potentially troublesome citizens into accepting community standards."*

at Cicuye and forced to surrender "five harquebuses, eleven swords, nineteen saddles, nine sets of horse armor, and a quantity of wearing apparel and bedding"; when de Sosa marched on the pueblo with a larger group to recover the goods and "exact submission from the Indians to our king," they found its residents waiting "in battle array" behind newly erected earthen bulwarks on the pueblo's terraces. Though the Spaniards circled the town several times and even attempted to initiate trade, Cicuye's residents were not to be appeased, and in the battle that soon ensued they greatly impressed their attackers with their valor and tactics. "None of them abandoned his section or trench," one of the Spaniards later wrote. "On the contrary, each one defended the post entrusted to him, without faltering in the least. Such intelligence among barbarians seemed incredible." Spanish firepower ultimately prevailed, however, and the invaders took control of the pueblo.

To their amazement, the Spanish soon discovered that they had won a deserted city, as the inhabitants gradually disappeared into underground passages so numerous and confusing that they seemed to the outsiders "a real labyrinth." One morning, the Spanish woke to discover that "at dawn . . . not a single inhabitant was to be found in the town." To the astonishment of their conquerors, who helped themselves to the substantial supplies of corn, beans, and flour to be found in the pueblo's well-stocked storehouses, the Indians "had abandoned their homes in the bitter cold of winter, with its strong winds and heavy snows, conduct which seemed incredible to us."

Upon closer inspection of the newly vacated town, the Spaniards found many things which seemed to them quite incredible, evidence of a prosperous and advanced civilization. Entering the passageways that had so baffled them, they discovered 16 very large and white-washed kivas. The town also had five plazas and two community water holes for bathing, as well as separate springs for drinking purposes. Food was in abundant supply; "each house had two or more rooms full of [corn], all of excellent quality," as well as different colors of beans and quantities of herbs, chili, and calabashes. Neither firewood nor lumber was lacking. The houses of the pueblo also contained farming implements and much pottery, "red, figured, and black, such as plates, bowls . . . salt containers, basins, and very beautiful cups," with some of the wares glazed.

The homes themselves were also a source of much admiration:

> The houses in this pueblo are built like military barracks, back to back, with doors opening out all around; and they are four or five stories high. There are no doors opening into the streets on the ground floors; the houses are entered from above by means of portable hand ladders and trap doors. Each floor of every house has three or four rooms, so that each house, as a whole counting from top to bottom, has fifteen or sixteen rooms, very neat and well

A distant view of Acoma, described by a Spanish soldier as "a rock out of reach, having steep sides in every direction, and so high that it was a very good musket that could throw a ball so high. There was only one entrance by a stairway built by hand, which began at the top of a slope which is around the foot of the rock."

whitewashed. Every house is equipped with facilities for grinding corn, including three or four grinding stones mounted in small troughs and provided with pestles; all is whitewashed.

After leaving Cicuye, the de Sosa party is thought to have traveled through Glorieta Pass and to have perhaps visited the Tesuque, Nambe, Cuyamuque, Pojoaque, and Jacona pueblos. Each pueblo was asked to pledge formal allegiance to the Spanish king, and a cross was erected in the village plaza to the sound of trumpets and harquebus shots. At each location, the Spanish were tremendously impressed with the Indians' architecture and agriculture, partic-

ularly their well-irrigated fields. Soon thereafter, a new Spanish force arrived in the area to arrest de Sosa, who had not secured a contract from the viceroy for his colonization scheme, and the Spanish returned to Mexico.

Though Espejo had failed in his mission, the Spanish did not abandon their efforts to colonize the north, and in 1598, Don Juan de Oñate, with 129 soldier-colonists, their wives and children, and 10 priests, arrived hungry in Pueblo country. The expedition had run out of supplies before reaching the Indian settlements, making for what had become by now the characteristic Spanish relationship with the Pueblos, as one Spaniard related:

We were in such extreme need that the governor found it necessary to send men ahead to the first pueblos with eighty pack animals to bring maize for our relief. They brought back the animals, all loaded, although it was against the wishes of the natives and to their great grief. As we had run short of food so far back, when we reached the said pueblos, we had to support ourselves by taking as much as we could from each one. Because of this and other annoyances, the Indians fear us so much that, on seeing us approach from afar, they flee to the mountains with their women and children, abandoning their homes, and so we take whatever we wish from them.

After once again taking official possession of the land for Spain, the governor and his followers proceeded north along the Rio Grande, passing pueblo after deserted pueblo before establishing themselves in the approximately 400

An archaeological excavation of a great Pueblo kiva, or underground ceremonial chamber. Most kivas were prominently located in the plaza of the pueblo. According to Henry Warner Bowden, "These underground cells usually had smooth floors of packed earth with a small hole or depression in the center. Benches ran around the perimeter. At one end there were often an altar, stone effigies, dance paraphernalia, and masks."

Zuni kachina masks used in religious ceremonies. Because of Spanish persecution, the Pueblos closely hid the details of their religious life from outsiders, a practice that has continued to the present day.

houses in the abandoned village of San Gabriel (across the river from the present-day settlement of San Juan). There, the Spaniards found themselves not as well suited for their new environment as were its native inhabitants; whereas the Pueblo settlements the Spanish had encountered seemed prosperous and healthy, the colonists lived in an atmosphere of scarcity and physical suffering. "The winter lasts eight months," wrote one,

and the cold is so intense that . . . the rivers freeze over and the Spaniards are always shivering by the fire. Moreover, there is a scarcity of firewood, which has to be brought six or eight leagues to the camp in wagons and carts. The wood is mostly cottonwood from the river valleys and it is so smoky that most of the women and children are in tears night and day, for they have nothing with which to provide light at night except these fires. . . . When winter is over there follow four months of summer as intensely warm as the winter is cold. So the saying there is that there are "eight months of winter and four of hell." The people leave their houses to sleep in their small vegetable gardens in order to escape the unbearable plague of bedbugs. Furthermore, there are an infinite number of field mice, which breed a species of lice, the pain from whose sting lasts for almost twenty-four hours. The mice eat the chile and peppers so fast that if the latter are not harvested in time the mice do not leave anything.

But the Spanish had no intention of trying to make this unforgiving landscape of mountain and desert support them. Instead, they planned to rely on the labor of its native inhabitants. Still chasing, in a fashion, the chimera of Cíbola, Oñate and his followers were quite certain that they would be able to obtain substantial mineral wealth from the discovery of mines, which they would make the Indians work; failing that, they would profit from what Oñate termed "the increase in vassals and tributes" from the Indians—slave labor and the forcible appropriation of food and such trade goods as turquoise, pearls, animal skins, and bird feathers.

Oñate's first order of business was therefore to reduce the populace of the Pueblo country to subjugation. On July 7, 1598, he gathered together the leaders of various communities at the pueblo of Santo Domingo, where they assembled in the great kiva. Through interpreters,

Oñate told them he had been sent by "the most powerful king and ruler in the world, Don Philip, King of Spain, who desired especially to serve God our Lord and to bring about the salvation of their souls, but wished also to have them as his subjects." As the king had sent the governor to this end at great expense and effort, Oñate explained, "it was greatly to their advantage that, of their own free will and in their own names and in those of the pueblos and republics . . . they render obedience and submission . . . and become his subjects and vassals." By so doing, they would not only live in peace and justice but also be "baptized and become good Christians . . . [and upon their death] would go to heaven to enjoy an eternal life of great bliss in the presence of god." The Pueblo elders, according to some sources, then conferred among themselves and with others before kneeling and kissing the hand of one of the priests as proof of their submission to the will of the king of Spain and the god of the Christians. Not long afterward, Oñate divided the Pueblo country into provinces and assigned them to the jurisdiction of the various priests, and on September 8 the church of St. John the Baptist was dedicated at San Juan pueblo.

Oñate's subsequent forays into the countryside in search of valuable minerals were thus provisioned by the pueblos along his route, with Acoma, Zuni, and Hopi villages generously supplying maize, water, game, and various other foodstuffs. As before, the villagers at the **Hopi pueblos welcomed the Spanish by scattering corn meal over the strangers** and their horses. At Jemez, the Indians even assisted them in getting their heavy cavalry armor and weapons up a difficult hill, but the Spaniards were shocked to discover one of the Pueblo chieftains wearing, as a medallion suspended by a cord from his neck, a paten belonging to one of the three ill-fated missionaries of the Rodríguez party. (A paten is a plate, made usually of silver or gold, used to carry the Eucharist in the Catholic mass.)

As Fray Diego de Mercado, a priest with a reputation for extreme piety, had foretold on the eve of the departure for the north of the Oñate expedition, the Spanish obsession with gold and other precious metals and gems spelled ultimate ruin. "God certainly does have great riches in these remote parts of New Mexico," Mercado had said as he watched the expedition take its leave, "but the present settlers are not to enjoy them, for God is not keeping these for them; and so it has been, for all the first people have died without enjoying them, and amidst great suffering, because they have always come with these desires and greediness for riches, which is the reason they went there to settle and spent their fortunes."

Having come to find a treasure in gold and silver, expecting to live on the labor of others, the colonists proved largely unwilling to do the work required to establish a self-supporting settlement—most specifically planting and tending fields and otherwise providing for a reliable source of food. Most were of a social class that regarded agricultural pursuits as beneath them,

and their efforts in New Mexico were characterized by lack of planning and extreme shortsightedness that was to condemn not only themselves, but also the indigenous population, to extreme hardship. Though they used forced native labor in their fields and gardens (as well as for tending livestock and in the repair of their houses), the crops were still never sufficient to feed the entire colony. Thus, the Indians were made as well to pay a sizable tribute to the Spanish.

Each month the soldiers went out, demanding goods from each native household. In a year's time the governor was paid "two thousand cotton blankets, which are a yard and a half long and almost as wide, five hundred dressed buckskins, five or six thousand *fanegas* [a Spanish unit of measurement] of maize and beans, and a very small number of fowls." Any resistance on the part of the Indians was put down with extreme cruelty; friars reported that Pueblo leaders were tortured and hanged "in order to induce the Indians to furnish corn." The burden of feeding the colonists was a heavy one for the Pueblos, whose extra stores, intended for lean times, were rapidly depleted. The "rainy day" for which the Indians had so carefully planned soon came, but in the form of drought—the cornfields dried up, and widespread famine ensued.

Many Indians (and even some Spaniards) starved, while others resorted to eating fruits and roots, or even ground cornstalks and charcoal mixed with seeds or withered, immature corn, har-

Pueblo pottery. Various design elements on such earthenware can be used to identify the village of origin.

vested before it even fully developed. To make matters worse, Oñate ordered the Spanish horses, which were similarly suffering from hunger, be allowed to run loose to forage, and the animals trampled and destroyed the remaining Pueblo fields. Spaniards and Indians alike grew frantic in their need, as revealed by the following stories—the first about a Spanish soldier and the second about an Indian mother—quoted by historians George P. Hammond and Agapito Rey in *The Rediscovery of New Mexico, 1580–1594*:

> [A Spanish official] went from this camp of San Gabriel in search of maize to some distant pueblos that had not been visited or plundered, hoping to find some provisions without vexing the natives too much. He was so desperate to find food lest the army perish that week that he tortured some Indians. The torture, inflicted with exquisite pain, led an Indian to confess where he had buried some maize in holes and caves. It was in such small amounts that, after some small ollas were unearthed, they found scarcely a fanega. The lids of these ollas were sealed with mud as if they contained the most precious liquor and as if the natives esteemed a kernel of maize more.
>
> Some of the natives, fleeing from hunger and privation, came and placed themselves at the mercy of the friars. Among them was an Indian woman, who died. She entered the house of a resident named Juan

López, asking for aid in the best manner she knew, to keep from starving. She offered, if given food, to accept baptism for herself and her eight-year-old son. They were both so weak, however, that the medicine and attention given them were not sufficient to save them from dying . . . although, before they died, they received the water of baptism and much faith and devotion.

The Spanish-imposed tribute of one blanket per family per year brought its own variety of suffering, especially in regions which did not raise cotton, as a Spanish soldier reported:

> Our men, with little consideration, took the blankets away from the Indian women, leaving them naked and shivering with cold. Finding themselves naked and miserable, they embraced their children tightly in their arms to warm and protect them, without making any resistance to the offenses done them, for they are an humble people, and in virtue and morality the best behaved thus far discovered.

Not surprisingly, pueblos were frequently abandoned at tribute time.

Hardship bred dissension among the colonists and more determined resistance on the part of those they oppressed. In 1599, the Indians defied Spanish soldiers who attempted to take provisions by force at the pueblo of Acoma; in the ensuing battle, hundreds of Indians and 11 Spaniards were killed. Two Franciscans who witnessed the incident at Acoma later testified to a commission of inquiry about various atrocities perpetrated there by their countrymen, including burning women and children alive.

Those Acoma residents who survived the massacre were dealt with severely, as a message from the Spanish to the other pueblos. Males over 25 years of age were sentenced to have one foot cut off and endure 20 years of personal servitude. Women over 12 years of age were sentenced to 20 years of servitude, and children under the age of 12 were placed in the care of either friars or colonists in order to be brought up as Christians and servants to the Spaniards.

But even subjugating and oppressing the Indians was harder work than many of the colonists had planned on, and when Oñate absented himself from the colony in 1601 for a reconnaissance trip east to the plains, three-quarters of the colony's disgruntled and hungry populace decamped back to Mexico. Reports of brutality and starvation continued to filter back to the viceroy in Mexico City, meanwhile, and in 1610 Oñate was recalled. With no apparent trove of gold and silver on the New Mexican horizon, the Spanish now turned their attention to the wealth of human souls available for harvest there. The consequences for the Pueblo would be no less profound. ▲

An elderly Pueblo man relaxes at Taos in 1981.

SLAVING
FOR
GOD

After Oñate's resignation, the Spanish outpost in the Pueblo country became a royal colony, supported by the Crown for the purpose of converting the indigenous peoples to Christianity. Civic authorities were entrusted with the protection of the friars and defense of the missions. Though known as the "Great Missionary Era" to students of the Spanish colony, the epoch was probably best remembered in the pueblos for its long days of intensive, forced labor—days in which the native communities struggled to supply both their own needs and the intruders' desires. It was largely Indian labor, for example, that built the Spaniards' new capital of Santa Fe. Workers were transported for this task from the pueblos; on the job, the Indians received only sparse rations of toasted maize or went hungry.

The loosely organized tributes of Oñate's day were now institutionalized in the form of the *encomendero* system.

Encomiendas, or land grants, were given to Spanish soldiers as restitution for five years of service. These grants often lay very close to the pueblos, though encomenderos were prohibited by law from living on the grants themselves. (This stricture was honored more often in the breech than in the observance, however; in addition, encomendero herds often destroyed Pueblo crops.) With the encomienda came regulated amounts of tribute—usually a cotton blanket and one fanega of corn from each Indian household—which were collected in May and October.

Spanish soldiers were also rewarded with *repartimiento*, or the right to the labor of those Indians residing near the *encomiendas*. In theory, workers were supposed to be compensated at a set rate of half a *real* [a unit of Spanish currency] a day, but in practice this Indian minimum wage was often ignored, and Pueblo herders, field hands, and ser-

The terraced, multi-level apartment dwellings at Zuni pueblo. Zuni is located much farther west in New Mexico than the Tanoan and Keresan pueblos and maintains several cultural distinctions; in general, Zuni is one of the more traditional pueblos.

vants were shortchanged or paid nothing at all for their services.

By 1621, Spanish abuse of the Pueblos was so extensive that the colonial authorities in Mexico City were forced to issue decrees regulating certain practices. Indian women, for example, were no longer to work as servants in Spanish households unless they went voluntarily *and* with their husbands; clearly, abuse of Pueblo women had become commonplace. The authorities also declared that henceforth Indian labor was not to inflict hardship upon the Pueblos: the number of workers to be drawn from any one pueblo was to be limited, labor was to be restricted to sowing and planting, and appropriate wages were to be paid. Nev-

ertheless, encomenderos persisted in summoning native workers at harvesttime (when their presence was most desperately required in their own fields), and rations and wages continued to be withheld.

Decrees notwithstanding, for the most part the Pueblos could expect little or no protection from the Spanish civil authorities. The soldiers tended to be a rough lot from frontier garrisons, and a disproportionate number of colonists were fugitives or convicted criminals. The vast majority of Spanish governors, whose responsibility it was to manage this unruly bunch, came to New Mexico with the express intent of personal financial enrichment, and Indian labor and resources were exploited in a variety of profit-making ventures to this end. For example, Governor Martinez de Baeza, who served in New Mexico from 1634 to 1637, forced the Indians to gather and transport piñon (the edible seeds of a pine tree native to the Southwest), to engage in extensive trade for hides, and to weave and paint large quantities of mantas and other textiles. Pueblos that did not raise cotton had to acquire it from other villages, and then were recompensed for the finished goods at prices a sixth or an eight of local values. Two years into his term, Baeza had accumulated sufficient goods to fill a nine-wagon caravan bound for New Spain.

Governor Luis de Rosas, who succeeded Baeza and served until 1641, expanded upon his predecessor's example by operating "sweatshops" in Santa Fe where Pueblo Indians toiled long hours alongside Apaches and Utes weaving all manner of textiles. Such operations attained their apex under the tenure of Bernardo Lopez de Medizabal, who governed from 1659 to 1661 and appropriated the labor of innumerable Pueblos to harvest, make, and transport various trade goods, including salt, maize, animal hides, shoes, stockings, shirts, and other items of apparel. Pueblo carpenters from Tiwa, Zia, Santa Ana, and Jemez even built the ox carts used

Women perform a Corn Dance at Santo Domingo pueblo. Pueblo dances and religious ceremonies are, according to Joe S. Sando, "carefully memorized prayerful requests for an orderly life, rain, good crops, plentiful game, pleasant days, and protection from the violence and the vicissitudes of nature."

for the great caravan that carried Lopez's booty to Mexico in 1661.

Though ostensibly more concerned with the Indians' well-being—they often complained of the excessive brutality of the soldiers—the Spanish clergy benefited as well from the labor of the Pueblos. By 1631, the number of priests in New Mexico had grown from the 8 who had accompanied Oñate to a total of 66, and the missionaries had expanded their efforts outward from the Tewa villages to those of the Keresans, the Tanos, and the Tiwas, and even to those of the Zuni and the Hopi. Triennial supply caravans arrived at the missions with regularity, bringing clothing, medicines, vestments, altar coverings, building materials, and more friars.

The friars customarily arrived in the pueblos with lay assistants and an escort of soldiers and then quickly set about their building program. Of primary importance was the church or chapel, which was augmented in the larger communities by a mission compound containing living quarters, workshops, stables, storerooms, and possibly a school. The labor was, of course, provided by village residents at great human cost. Large roof beams of pine had to be transported from distant forested mountains; in the outlying pueblos, church walls were often constructed of sandstone slabs set in mud.

The religious instruction the Indians received was simple. Regular attendance at services was required, and the Indians were admonished to venerate the cross and respect the clergy. Basic prayers and the sacraments were also taught. Native rites, sexual promiscuity, and "sorcery" were adamantly denounced. The padres also frequently attempted to instruct the Indians in the catechism, music, Latin, painting, blacksmithing, carpentry, weaving, and a dozen other subjects. Some Indians were taught to be actors and performed in little plays that carried a religious theme.

Mission activities were by no means limited to conversion and spiritual guidance. The friars managed substantial herds and extensive fields, which ostensibly served to feed the native population in times of famine and to provide income for ecclesiastical furnishings. The Pueblos were expected to supply the clergy with shepherds, farmhands, horsemen, cooks, gardeners, and maids in addition to the interpreters, sacristans, bell-ringers, choir members, and *cantor mayors* [the lead singer in a church choir] required for routine mission affairs. So extensive were the mission operations that when Lopez de Medizabal raised the Indian minimum wage in 1659 to a full real day (plus food) and refused to exempt the clergy, the economic repercussions for the friars were devastating: nine missions claimed losses of more than 6,000 head of stock due to the cutback in Indian labor.

Resentful of competition with his own enterprises, Lopez often charged the friars with having greater interest in the economic welfare of the missions than in spiritual leadership. When the guardian of the Jumano pueblo, Diego de Santander, wrote the governor

An Edward S. Curtis photograph of Zuni gardens. The early Spanish settlers of New Mexico soon came to depend on the skill of the Pueblos as agriculturalists.

lamenting the poor attendance of the Indians at mass, Lopez caustically replied that perhaps they failed to attend because they knew the "continual toil that the mass costs them." Lopez sarcastically expressed doubt regarding the Indians' knowledge of Catholicism but was confident that the converts were well versed in how "to guard and herd an infinite number of livestock, to serve as slaves, and to fill barns with grain, cultivated and harvested with their blood, not for their humble homes, but for those of the friars."

The friars were generally humorless and unrelenting disciplinarians with little understanding or tolerance of native tradition. For the slightest offenses —failure to attend mass, for example—Indians had their heads shaved, were whipped, or were detained in stocks. A particularly brutal incident of punishment took place in 1655 at the Hopi settlements, where a priest named Salvador de Guerra beat an Indian until he was "bathed in blood," then salved the Indian's wound with "burning turpentine." The Indian died soon thereafter; his offense was engaging in an "act of idolatry," by which was meant practicing the Pueblos' traditional religion. It was further charged that Guerra had dealt with the "immoral conduct" of Pueblo boys and girls in a similar fashion and had required Indians to weave cotton and woolen mantas, whipping those who failed to meet the established quotas in a specified amount of time.

Zuni women carry water in their distinctive jars. The Zunis are especially well known for their pottery, which is usually chalky white with large brown-black designs.

Other questions were raised concerning the moral conduct of the clergy. Perhaps the most notorious case was that of Fray Diego de Parraga of Tajique. In 1660, a resident of that pueblo accused the friar of having had an affair with his wife over a period of three years and of having fathered a child by her. Similar complaints were submitted by a San Cristóbal woman, and during the course of an investigation over 20 Indian women testified regarding incidents of misconduct perpetrated by the priest. Though Parraga was latter acquitted, the inquiry caused considerable embarrassment and fueled already rampant gossip about the earthly appetites of many of the missionaries.

Even those friars with good intentions often offended the Indians through their ignorance or indifference to native tradition. Traditional Pueblo society practiced a strict division of labor, as one missionary observed:

> Among these nations it is the custom for the women to build the walls; and the men spin and weave their mantas, and go to war and the chase; and if we try to oblige some man to build a wall, he runs away from it, and the women laugh.

In their zealousness to have God's kingdom built with all due speed, the friars often ignored such traditional strictures.

By 1631, missionaries were stationed in 25 different pueblos, and 90 chapels had been constructed. One of the missionaries, Fray Alonso de Benavides, painted a rosy picture of the Franciscans' progress, claiming complete conversion and Christian loyalty for thousands of the newly baptized:

> [The Indians] are so well doctrinated and [good] Christians that when we ring the bell for Mass and the [teaching of the] Doctrine, they all come with the greatest cleanliness and neatness . . . and enter the church to pray, as if they were Christians of very long standing . . . and the choristers in the chapels . . . sing every day in the church, at their hours, the Morning Mass, High Mass, and Vespers, with great punctuality. And all make confession in their [own] tongue, and prepare themselves for the confession, studying out their sins and bringing them marked on knotted threads. And they are always of notable submission and affection toward the Religious who minister to them . . . and . . . have a notable affection for . . . the things of the Church, which they attend with notable love and devotion.

But even the scant historical record that remains demonstrates that the Pueblos often exhibited a less-than-devoted attitude towards the mission efforts. Their displeasure and contempt was manifested in a number of ways, both personal and collective, and both humorous and violent. As early as 1623 the residents of Jemez rose in revolt against the policies of Fray Jeronimo de Zarate Salmeron, who had resettled the Jemez villages into a large pueblo at the convent of San José, and killed him. Such forced resettlements occurred frequently and often resulted in a temporary loss or reduction of the harvest—a disastrous consequence for a pueblo such as Jemez, which was already severely taxed by Navajo raids. Diego de San Lucas, a successor of Salmeron, was also killed. In 1632, the residents of Zuni killed friars Francisco de Letrado and Martin de Arvide, only three years after the Franciscans had taken up residence in the Zuni villages. As at Jemez, a punitive expedition was sent to calm the rebellion, with no success: the Indians had taken refuge on Corn Mountain, where they remained until 1635. By 1640, a friar had been killed at Taos, and similar unrest had taken hold at Picuris. By that time, the inhabitants at Taos, Jemez, Zuni, and Hopi were regarded as being so rebellious that service there was considered to be dangerous "banishment" by encomenderos and was in fact often used as punishment by governors for insubordinates or other troublemakers.

In a less dramatic fashion, the Indians resisted the missionaries with wit and humor. Indian translators might render the friar's words in hilarious obscenities, and at Awatovi a Hopi named Juan took advantage of the priest's absence to summon, by the ringing of the mission bells, the inhabitants of the pueblo to the church, where he conducted a solemn parody of the mass, with himself in the priest's role. At Taos, an Indian named Francisco was said to have appeared in a pueblo dance in the vestments of the community's martyred friar, Pedro de Miranda.

Although the Hispanicized names of the Indians mentioned above provide some indication of the inroads made by Spanish culture in the Pueblo country, there was simultaneously an even greater indication of the determination of the Indians to retain the most important elements of their traditional culture—namely, the continued practice of their ancient religion. Despite his optimistic assessments, Benavides himself conceded that the Pueblos continued to conduct their traditional ceremonies, citing Indian offerings of cornmeal to the heads of slain animals, to the scalps of dead enemies, to rivers to be fished—rituals intended to maintain the favor of the Creator by indicating their respect for the spirits of the earth and the animal kingdom, thereby ensuring a successful harvest or hunt. Though the Spanish did their best to prevent the Pueblos from dancing or engaging in any of their other ceremonial rituals, it became clear to the Franciscans that nominal Pueblo participation in Catholic ritual did not preclude adherence to older native religious tenets, and that the friars had not supplanted village priests and medicine men. Kivas and village plazas, not churches and mission compounds, remained the focus of village life. The Christian faith was, if accepted to any degree, regarded as a supplement, not an alternative, to a religion that had served the Pueblos and their ancestors well.

Curiously, native religion benefited from the ever-increasing tension between the Spanish church and state.

Kosa from San Juan pueblo. The clowns served to entertain as well as to enforce social conformity. According to Henry Warner Bowden, the clowns "served as the local police force, dealing with social deviance to ensure the smooth operation of village life."

Colonists accused the friars of amassing personal wealth at the expense of the Pueblos and charged the Franciscans with sexual depravity and other offenses against the indigenous population. The missionaries made counterclaims of mistreatment at the hands of secular authorities and reported abuses of Indian labor on the part of royal governors. Realizing that the friars were intent upon maintaining strict Catholic discipline in the pueblos, civil officials frequently retaliated in these disputes by encouraging indigenous practices. For example, an early governor of New Mexico, Juan de Eulate, who ruled from 1618 to 1625, took action to protect Indian priests, who were referred to by the missionaries as "sorcerers" (hechiceros). His interpreter for the Tiwa pueblos and encomendero of San Lazaro, Juan Gomez, went so far as to assure the residents of that pueblo that he would bring back an order from Mexico ensuring them the right to "follow their old ways."

It was Governor Lopez, however, who most flagrantly defied the church. Lopez went beyond mere tolerance of religious rites in the pueblos to the public sanction of indigenous dances in the streets of the Spanish capital of Santa Fe, ostensibly for the purpose of firsthand research into native customs. Concluding that the sacred rituals were harmless "Indian nonsense" (boberia de indios), he gave permission for public dances in all the pueblos, where on occasion the Indian dancers were even joined by their Spanish neighbors.

Despite Spanish attempts to the contrary, the Pueblos were also able to maintain a relative degree of autonomy in their civic affairs during the 17th century. One of Costano de Sosa's first acts upon entry into any given pueblo was to name civil government representatives in each community, and by the 1620s the Spanish offices of governor, lieutenant governor, *aguacil*, and *mayordomo* had been established in pueblo communities, complemented by the church offices of sacristan and *fiscale*. The municipal government of each pueblo was to serve as the representative body with which the Spanish authorities would conduct business.

The Spanish, of course, intended the establishment of government institutions as another means whereby to impose their civilization on the Pueblos, but as the historian Edward P. Dozier has pointed out, the Indians were able to subvert these institutions to serve as concealment for their own traditional governing structures:

> [Pueblo] officers were expected to co-operate with Spanish civil and church officials in compelling their members to comply with the civilizing and Christianizing efforts of the Spaniards. But the fact unknown to the Spaniards was that the Indians who filled these positions were chosen by native priests and were individuals who owed primary allegiance to native ceremonial life.

The system of pueblo government established by the Spanish thereby served as a convenient facade behind which the more important and vital organization of native priests carried out the social and religious functions of the pueblo.

As a result of active Indian resistance, Pueblo nonmaterial culture and daily life seems to have changed little during the Great Missionary Era. Pueblo farmers tended a variety of new crops in the mission gardens—wheat, melons, apples, peaches, pears, tomatoes, and chile—but these foods were largely intended for the clergy and the Spanish elite and had a negligible effect upon the native diet. Pueblo Indians were denied the use of horses or firearms, and the introduction of sheep meant a burden—of additional forced labor at the loom—not a boon to the Pueblos. According to Dozier, the new manual skills learned by the Pueblos in the mission workshops were probably regarded by them as cursed innovations of great detriment and little value:

> The introduced crafts meant simply additional work for the Indians: weaving in wool, blacksmithing (iron, tin, copper, bronze, and silver), and wood-working. Along with all of these introductions went an assorted complex of tools and equipment like saddles, bridles, harnesses, metal knives, sickles, needles, axes, and so forth. The Pueblo Indian during the 17th century was kept so busy working to produce enough for his support and the support of a substantial part of the colonial population that he must have viewed these new additions to his culture as techniques to exploit his labor rather than as items to enrich his economy.

As the Pueblo agricultural techniques were superior to anything with which the Spanish colonists were familiar, the Indians continued to use them; as metal tools were hard to come by in the early days in New Mexico, it is doubtful that they augmented native implements significantly. Pueblo building technology, save for the introduction of adobe brick, also remained essentially the same.

But many profound changes were wrought by the intruders upon the Pueblo communities, however. Epidemics of European diseases—primarily smallpox—swept through the villages every 10 to 12 years. In 1640 a major outbreak took the lives of 3,000 persons, over 10 percent of the Pueblo population. Raids by Apache and Navajo Indians further diminished the Pueblo populace. These raids were often stepped up in times of drought or general scarcity, when Spanish crops made tempting targets, but they were also motivated by a desire for revenge for Spanish slaving expeditions. Apaches and Navajos were also often seized when they came peacefully to trade in the pueblos; the captives were then either pressed into service in the workshops and ranches or were sent to New Spain to be sold as slaves.

Pueblo communities, especially those on the frontiers, suffered the inevitable repercussions of this unprovoked treachery on the part of Spanish slave entrepreneurs, sustaining attack after attack until entire communities had to be abandoned. At the same time, the Spanish attempted to exploit Pueblo trade relations with the Apaches and Navajos by providing the easternmost communities with knives to trade for buffalo hides, meat, and lard. An annual trade fair was held at Pecos, for example, where Apaches had long exchanged their buffalo wares for Pueblo cloth and maize. Transactions could also be conducted by expeditions traveling to the plains, and Pueblo leader Esteban Clemente, who frequently visited the Apaches of the Siete Rios, was known to have been enlisted by Lopez for just such purposes.

Famines associated with periods of drought caused as much human misery

Tiny religious figurines from Tesuque pueblo, the southernmost of the Tewa pueblos, just 10 miles north of the city of Santa Fe.

as Apache raids and disease. In 1668, for example, 450 Indians died at the eastern pueblo of Las Humanas; no crops had been harvested there for three years. Fray Francisco de Ayeta described an even worse period of want and suffering in New Mexico that began in 1670 "and compelled the Spanish inhabitants and Indians alike to eat the hides that they had and the straps of the carts, preparing them for food by soaking and washing them and toasting them in the fire (like) maize and boiling them with herbs and roots."

Spanish cruelty, disease, famine, warfare, and other manifestations of cultural disruption all contributed to a significant reduction of the Pueblo population, which numbered an estimated 50,000 at the beginning of the 17th century and only 17,000 some seven decades later. Dozens of pueblos had been abandoned since Oñate's entrada almost a century earlier, and the number of Spanish colonists had grown to about 3,500.

Such catastrophic social upheaval provoked the Pueblos to a more fervent embrace of their own traditions, especially their religion, and a more outright resistance to the Spanish, especially the missionaries. A harmonious social order, good weather, and bountiful harvests were the ends the Pueblos hoped to gain from faithful adherence to their native rituals; since the coming of the Spanish, the Pueblos had known war, drought, and famine. To many of the Indians, it became clear that the difficulties besetting their culture arose from

their acceptance, even if it was not always truly genuine, of certain elements of the Spanish religion and culture. The result, beginning in the 1670s, was a resurgent Pueblo commitment to their traditional beliefs, matched by an increased Spanish determination to eradicate native practices. Friars seized kivas, destroyed ritual masks, dance costumes, and prayer sticks, and imprisoned Pueblo religious leaders on charges of witchcraft. In the most notorious incident, in 1675, 47 Pueblos were arrested on charges of witchcraft and sorcery; three of them were then publicly hanged in their home pueblos, while the rest were severely beaten.

While the Spanish oppression was intensifying, the Pueblos, under the leadership of a Tewa Indian from the pueblo of San Juan named Popé, were, in contrast to the usual independence of action practiced by the various communities, planning a unified uprising to drive the Spanish from New Mexico. The rebellion began on August 10, 1680. The widely scattered Spanish settlements along the Rio Grande valley were quickly overrun, and by August 21, 1680, the last Spanish holdouts abandoned the city of Santa Fe. Spanish casualties, except among the missionaries, were relatively light—an estimated 350 killed; the Pueblos wished only to drive the Spanish from their lands, not annihilate them. Most of the Pueblo fury was directed at the most tangible symbols of the Spanish religion—the mission buildings themselves, most of which were torched, and records of religious cere-

Don Diego de Vargas reconquered New Mexico for Spain in 1693, although his claim that he accomplished this feat "without wasting a single ounce of powder, unsheathing a sword, or without costing the Royal Treasury a single maravedi" was considerably exaggerated.

monies such as baptisms, first communions, and marriages, which were also destroyed. According to the historian Henry Warner Bowden, "Famine, disease, and attacks from marauders convinced most Pueblos that they had seriously erred in accepting elements of the intruders' religion alongside their own. . . . The revolt was the concerted act of a people determined to resist Christian civilization because it posed a direct threat to their culture and religion."

But the great Pueblo rebellion was ultimately only a holding action against the inevitable. Widespread drought and famine continued even after the Spanish left, and the abandonment of their garrisons made the settlements that much more attractive a target for the Apaches; many pueblos had to be abandoned. The Pueblos themselves, accustomed to a tradition of community autonomy, found it difficult to remain unified, particularly after Popé died in 1688. Accordingly, in 1692, the Spanish general Diego de Vargas—summoned, based on one Pueblo tradition, by a delegation of Indians who had asked the Spanish to return—reclaimed Santa Fe with a small force. Although sporadic Pueblo resistance continued, at times pitting those Indians who supported the Spanish against those who opposed them, by 1696 all the remaining inhabited pueblos, except for those of the Hopis, had again been subdued. ▲

*Women at the watering hole at Acoma pueblo. It is estimated that
Acoma pueblo was built atop the mesa there around the year 1000.*

ERA
OF
ACCOMODATION

Less than two years after the death of de Vargas, the new Spanish governor of New Mexico, Francisco Cuervo y Valdez, summoned Pueblo leaders to the Spanish capital for a historic meeting. Assembled on that cold January day in 1706 were all the Pueblo governors (save for Hopi) and various Spanish officials. The ostensible purpose of the meeting was to introduce Alfonso Rael de Aguilar, the recently appointed "Protector General" of the Indians, to the Pueblos, but the meeting's true significance was as a symbolic inauguration of a new era of mutual cooperation and good relations. The Pueblos had come to realize that they could not drive the Spanish permanently from their homeland, while the colonists had been made painfully aware that their physical survival in New Mexico depended on alliance with the Pueblos in the form of economic and military cooperation. The Spanish recognized that their economy and very

survival was dependent on barter with the Pueblos, who also helped them fend off raids from the Apaches, Utes, and Comanches; at the same time, the Pueblos began to slowly and selectively assimilate those aspects of Spanish material culture that had been observed to be beneficial.

Clearly, both Pueblo and Spaniard had learned valuable lessons from the bitter events of the previous century. The encomienda system was abolished. Institutionalized tribute and forced labor were replaced by extensive trade with the Pueblos for food, fuel, and clothing. A standardized value scale was established whereby potential disagreements could be avoided: the value of a horse or blanket was fixed at being worth so many fanegas of Pueblo maize or beans, and so forth.

Old abuses were, of course, not eradicated completely. In 1707 San Juan pueblo complained to the governor of

New Mexico that Spanish officials exercised dictatorial control over the inhabitants, illegally forcing them to work on Sundays. The following year the viceroy felt compelled to issue an order prohibiting Spanish officials from extorting land and services from the Pueblos. But, whereas such behavior had been taken for granted before the revolt, after 1700 official Spanish policy attempted to avoid antagonizing Pueblo communities, and complaints were reviewed seriously.

Meanwhile, the Pueblo survivors of encomienda and mission servitude put their newly-acquired skills to use for their home communities. According to Edward P. Dozier, the well-organized and efficient Pueblo villages of the 18th and 19th centuries owed much to Indian apprentices who had become highly proficient herdsmen, cowboys, and blacksmiths—trades forced upon them by Spanish colonization. Fray Dominguez's 1776 description of the households at Tesuque reveals the subtle synthesis of tradition and innovation that emerged in the pueblos over the course of the 18th century:

> The houses of which the pueblo is composed are adobe and like other Indian houses in these parts. . . . The entrance to some houses is by little doors on the street; others have ladders, and some of these ascend to a door which resembles a little window torn in the wall of the upper apartment. . . . The fastenings are a wooden lock and key.

A man's cloth shirt, probably from Jemez pueblo. Some Pueblo apparel revealed the influence of the Plains tribes with whom they traded.

> The ceilings are quite low. Some dwellings are more spacious than others, and as a general rule all are poorly whitewashed. . . . The kitchen is in any room the owner pleases and it contains several metates (three or four) fixed to the floor with mud (these are generally found after this fashion in the houses of both Indians and settlers), all boxed in with boards, and divided from one another by another small board set crosswise so that the wheat, maize, or other things being ground by hand may not spill, nor may the contents of one metate get mixed with those of another.
>
> The interior decoration of these houses varies according to the owner, but they usually have two or three prints, a wooden cross, some kind of chest, either plain or painted. The arms of the men and the harnesses of the horses are hung from

stakes, and there are some *matlacahuitl* (a pole and net or rope used to hang skins/clothing out of reach of vermin) on which, like the secondhand dealers of Mexico, they hang their skins of buffalo, lion, wolf, sheep, and other animals, and also their cloaks if they have any, and the rest of the clothing belonging to both men and women. Outside are the little ovens, like those of the bakeshops, and the henhouses. Around the pueblo, but not very near to it, there are corrals to confine livestock of various kinds, and small corrals for fattening pigs.

Peach and apricot trees quietly took their place next to native corn and beans. Dominguez marveled that farmers at San Ildefonso (the name of the pueblo itself indicates a blend of Spanish and Native American cultures) tended 10 orchards of two varieties of peaches and produced melons and watermelons "better and larger than those from the Tierra Caliente." Except at Zuni, oxen had come to be used to ease the burden of tilling the land, and the labor required to maintain irrigation ditches was at times shared with Spanish settlers.

Planting at the pueblos was intensive

The northernmost pueblo is at Taos and is at least 600 years old.

A harvest dance at Picuris. The Pueblo ceremonial calendar covers the entire year. The success of the Pueblos in retaining their land is perhaps the single largest reason why they have also been able to maintain their traditional religion.

and yielded a good return—no doubt because Pueblo farmers were once again assured that the fruits of their labor would go to feed their own and that any surplus would replenish long-depleted storehouses. Although the friars continued to solicit supplies from villagers, these contributions, whether from Indian or Spaniard, were now on a voluntary basis. Apparently only Laguna, Acoma, and Zuni complied to any degree with such requests; the remaining pueblos offered goods to the clergy only in the form of barter. A typical donation consisted of such items as a sheep, frijoles, broad beans, eggs, lard, salt, flour, a tallow candle, and milk. Maize was purchased from the pueblos for the Spanish troops in Santa Fe; Santo Domingo and Cochiti supplied the Spanish towns with lettuce, chili, garlic, and other vegetables. Acoma, Laguna, and Zuni bred flocks of sheep for wool, which was woven into blankets both for personal use and for trade. The Rio Grande villages raised cotton to be used in cloth for the same purposes. The farmers of these latter pueblos seem to have been continually bothered by Spanish livestock, which grazed extensively on the open range and frequently wandered into Pueblo fields. Spanish governors generally lent a sympathetic ear to the resultant complaints, often ordering compensation for damages incurred. In addition to the lands recognized by the Spanish as belonging to the Indians, the Pueblos also sometimes worked mission lands as sharecroppers, and in at least one instance the natives of Santa Ana pueblo succeeded in purchasing land from the Spanish.

The changes in economic relations between the Pueblos and the missions in the 18th century reflected a decline in the status of the Catholic church in Pueblo country after the great revolt. Though de Vargas reestablished the missions in 1695, they never regained the vitality or importance they had enjoyed during the early colonial period. By 1776, there were only 20 priests in all of New Mexico, and several pueblos had no resident missionary assigned to them. No new building programs were implemented, and the friars struggled to recruit sufficient labor to keep existing structures maintained and in good repair. For the entire 18th century, the missionaries claimed to have succeeded in converting only 4,000 to 5,000 Pueblos to Christianity.

And even the Spanish recognized that the "converted" Indians' adherence to Christianity was essentially superficial. Just as the Pueblos learned how to speak Spanish in order to conduct trade and otherwise maintain relations with the newcomers, yet maintained their native languages, they adopted the trappings of Catholicism while never straying inwardly from their native faith. (Sociologists call this process compartmentalization.) "[The Pueblos] adjusted to the foreigners' control over secular matters whenever necessary but rarely allowed Christianity to penetrate the private sphere of their religious sensibilities. . . . If the Pueblos adopted elements of Hispanic Christianity, it was only the externals of the European faith, to appease the missionaries and keep them at arm's length," writes Henry Warner Bowden. Fray Dominguez recognized that the Pueblos' grasp of Catholicism was consciously superficial and their participation in its rites hesitant and minimal: "Their repugnance and resistance to most Christian acts is evident, for they perform the duties pertaining to the Church under compulsion, and there are usually many omissions." Dominguez complained also that the majority of Pueblos preferred to be called by "appellations according to the custom handed down from their ancestors" rather than by the names of Christian saints given them in baptism, and that, indeed, when called by their Christian names "they usually have their joke among themselves, repeating the saint's name to each other as if in ridicule."

Indians would not participate in the sacrament of confession except on their deathbed because the interpreters employed—Spanish priests remained reluctant to learn the Indian languages—were from the same village and would broadcast their sins. A priest named Fray Joaquin de Jesus Ruiz, who was stationed at Jemez in the latter decades of the 18th century, complained of the frivolity of the Pueblos during mass, including constant "gossip" among the women, roughhousing among the youths, and a "nude" male Indian "with his private parts uncovered performing many obscene acts" during a certain prayer.

Though the Spanish did not report any significant rise in what a Bishop Tamaron called the "use or practice of formal idolatry," there is little doubt that the 18th century was a time of continued resurgence of native religious practices, which were generally kept hidden from Christian eyes. Tamaron, for example, was frustrated by the inability of his friars to eliminate kivas from the pueblos, and Dominguez's detailed description of the preparations undergone by the participants in a corn dance indicates a ceremonial life whose richness and strength was showing no sign of abatement:

> Just as our Spaniards bathe before putting on their gala finery, so these Indians bathe before bedizening themselves with filthy earths of different colors . . . with which they paint their nakedness from head to foot, covering their private parts with a breechcloth like a loin cloth. They usually paint half the body lengthwise with one color and half with another, or sections of the whole body in the same way.
>
> One foot, one color, the other, another; one leg one color, the other, another; one thigh in one way, the other in another; and so bit by bit they reach the head. . . . Moreover, they tie a tortoise shell to one leg, hanging near it many little cloven hooves of deer, sheep, or similar animals, so that all this rings and sounds with movement of the body like little bells. They also tie on some of these cascabels, or other small bells, and it all serves to make music.
>
> Although the women bathe, they do not undress, or paint anything except their cheeks with carmine, using make-up to supply what nature failed to give them. Both women and men go barefoot, let their hair hang loose. The men tie a small handful of macaw feathers on their heads, and the women put on some little painted boards trimmed with a few feathers and latticed with agave fiber. . . . They put on good blankets and hang about their necks as many rosaries, crosses, or medals as they can, and all hanging from ribbons.

The dance itself, Dominguez wrote, was conducted against the backdrop of the "metered prose" of the chorus and the soft beating of the drum.

Native belief and tradition was stronger in the western pueblos—Zuni,

Acoma, and Laguna—than in those along the Rio Grande. Although missions were reestablished at both Zuni and Acoma subsequent to the Pueblo Revolt, there was difficulty keeping a priest in residence at either location throughout the 18th century. Resistance to Christianity was even more unyielding at the Hopi settlements, which in the 18th century became home to many displaced Pueblo rebels from other villages who were steadfastly determined to have little to do with the Spanish.

But if religion remained a subject of much misunderstanding and mistrust between the Pueblos and the Spanish, military necessities brought the two peoples closer together. By the 1730s, the troublesome Navajos, Utes, and Apaches had been joined in their raids on Spanish and Pueblo settlements by an even more fearsome enemy, the Comanches. As the Spanish presidio at Santa Fe maintained a fighting force of less than 100 men—a number clearly inadequate to defend the widely-scattered Spanish settlers—Spanish authorities thus relied upon Pueblo auxiliaries to hold the raiding tribes at bay.

For the Pueblos, perhaps the most significant consequences of the Spanish need for their military assistance was that Spanish restrictions on Indian ownership of firearms and especially of horses became impractical. By 1752, the pueblos of Laguna, Acoma, and Zuni had more horses than any single Spanish village, and Laguna alone could claim almost as many steeds as all the Spanish settlers combined. At San Juan, in 1760,

Bishop Tamaron noted with some surprise that the Pueblos had become so adept as horsemen that they used the animals to cross the flood-swollen Rio Grande. "In astonishment I asked whether canoes could navigate there," wrote Tamaron. "They [the Pueblos] replied that everyone crossed on horseback. . . . They ride the horses bareback; they are now expert; and in this fashion old men and women, boys and girls, and all kinds of people crossed without a single incident."

Another consequence was closer day-to-day relations between the two peoples. Initially, Pueblo military divisions were segregated from the Spanish soldiers; livestock and camps were kept separate as well. This practice was abandoned in the latter half of the century. By that time, Pueblos often comprised 75 to 85 percent of "Spanish" expeditions, serving not only as warriors but also as spies, scouts, interpreters, and messengers. Although the officers of such expeditions were always Spanish, Pueblo war captains exerted command over their own men. Several Pueblo Indians made names for themselves as formidable leaders in the campaigns against enemy tribes, among them Domingo Romero of Tesuque, Don Felipe Chisto of Pecos, and Jose Narajo of Santa Clara.

In military campaigns, the Pueblos offered the Spanish more than manpower. Pueblo villages served as rendezvous points and supplied the fighting troops with food and equipment. For their service and aid, the Pueblos expected in return to achieve a modicum of physical security, to recover captive loved ones and valuable livestock, and to share in war booty and other privileges. While necessity demanded a higher level of tolerance on the part of the Spanish, there were some Pueblo war practices that the Spanish continued to regard as unacceptable, foremost among them the taking of scalps and the scalp ceremonies directed by the Pueblo war societies.

Despite the frequent warfare, trade between the Pueblos, the Spanish, and the other Indian peoples of the region continued. In some instances, exchanges were made on neutral ground with distrustful caution, as was the case with a group of Apaches who intercepted Bishop Tamaron's party in 1760:

> On May 11 it was freezing at dawn. On this day we reached the dread site of Robleo, where we spent the night. It is an unavoidable stopping place. . . . The place is frightening, and the danger one runs there increases this aspect, for most travelers are attacked by infidel Indians, which is a very frequent occurrence at that place. . . . A little farther on . . . we found a black cross about a vara and a half high and as thick as a man's thumb at the side of the road, and at its foot a deerskin sack containing two pieces of fresh venison and a deerskin. The Apaches, who must have been in the Dona Ana sierra, put it there. By this means they indicated that they were at peace and that we should give them food and buy the deerskin. The experienced

> guides gave this interpretation. And therefore they left a knife in exchange for the deerskin and and kept putting pieces of bread and tobacco leaf in the sack. And a short distance away, for we were on the lookout, two Indians on horseback were sighted. They were coming to see what had been left for them.

Formalized annual trade fairs were held in other locations, usually in late summer or fall. Taos, Pecos, and Picuris were often visted by the Comanches and Utes, while the Navajos frequented Santa Clara, Jemez, and Acoma. Fighting was suspended long enough for each side to acquire the specialty items of their enemies. The Taos fair, which was placed under the jurisdiction of local authorities in 1723, was described by Tamaron in 1760:

> They come every year to the trading, or fairs. The governor comes to those fairs, which they call *rescates* (barter, trade), every year with the majority of his garrison and people from all over the kingdom. They bring captives to sell, pieces of chamois, many buffalo skins, and, out of the plunder they have obtained elsewhere, horses, muskets, shotguns, munitions, knives, meat, and various other things. Money is not current at these fairs, but exchange of one thing for another, and so those people get provisions.

Sixteen years later, Fray Dominguez found the Taos fair largely unchanged:

continued on page 73

THE OLDEST ARCHITECTS

They are reminders that "civilization" was not a gift bestowed on the native inhabitants of North America by their native conquerors, and testimony to the creativity, ingenuity, and practicality of a people. They inspired greedy newcomers to dream of gold and mythical treasure, and they convinced these outsiders that their inhabitants were less "savage" than their more nomadic neighbors. Above all, the homes and other buildings constructed by the Pueblos constitute the most characteristic material evidence of the enduring virtues of their culture.

Pueblo architecture was in all likelihood a cultural inheritance from their forebears, the Anasazi, or Ancient Ones. It was the Anasazi who first built, often in the recesses of cliffs or atop defensible mesas, the huge "apartment" buildings of numerous rooms and multiple stories that inspired the legend of the Seven Cities of Cibola. Though still made of adobe, sandstone, or tufa, later Pueblo dwellings tended to be smaller; the low-slung, flat-roofed style characteristic of Pueblo dwellings along the Rio Grande continues to inspire much Southwestern architecture.

Metates—stones used for grinding corn—inside an Indian ruin. Corn was the Pueblos' most important staple; most Pueblo dwellings would include rooms for its storage.

Ancient Indian petroglyphs. The Pueblos had a highly developed and extremely complex civilization long before Europeans came to the New World.

Anasazi ruins at the Hovenweep National Monument in Utah.

The famous White House Ruin in Canyon de Chelly, Arizona. No one knows for certain why the Anasazi migrated from their canyons in the Four Corners area. Raids by hostile tribes and shortages of water and wood are the most likely explanation.

Anasazi ruins in Mesa Verde National Park. During the golden age of the Anasazi, which lasted from the 11th to the 14th century, they abandoned their mesa-top villages in favor of impregnable cliffside dwellings.

The north pueblo at Taos, which is about 600 years old.

Modern doors and windows on a home in the north pueblo at Taos.

70

The structure to the left of the front door of this home in Taos pueblo is a bread oven made of adobe.

The entranceway to the courtyard of the old church at Taos
pueblo. The Pueblo cultural heritage today includes many
traditions of Hispanic origin, among them a nominal belief
in Roman Catholicism. In recent years, some inhabitants
of Taos have become practitioners of the peyote religion.

continued from page 64

When they are on their good behavior, or at peace, they enter Taos to trade. At this fair they sell buffalo hides, "white elkskins," horses, mules, buffalo meat, pagan Indians (of both sexes, children and adults) whom they capture from other nations. . . . They also sell good guns, pistols, powder, balls, tobacco, hatchets, and some vessels of yellow tin (some large, others small) shaped like the crown of the friars' hats, but the difference is that the top of the hat is the bottom of the vessel. These have an handle made of an iron hoop to carry them. . . . The Comanches usually sell to our people at this rate: a buffalo hide for a *belduque*, or broad knife made entirely of iron which they call a trading knife here; "white elkskin" (it is the same (buffalo) hide, but softened like deerskin), the same; for a very poor bridle, two buffalo skins or a vessel like those mentioned; the meat for maize or corn flour; an Indian slave, according to the individual, because if it is an Indian girl from twelve to twenty years old, two good horses and some trifles in addition, such as a short cloak, a horse cloth, a red lapel are given; or a she-mule and a scarlet cover, or other things are given for her.

Days after the trade fairs had dispersed, the raids would resume. By the 1770s the attacks had become insufferable. "In addition to the outrages and hostilities they commit against every kind of traveler on the roads," Domin-guez wrote about the hostile Indians, "they enter the pueblos, steal from them all the horses and mules they find, make captives of the little ones who fall into their hands, and leave their parents, if not completely dead, without the better half of their lives, which is their children." The population of Santa Fe doubled as a result of the attacks, as Spanish settlers left the countryside for the safety of numbers. Some Spanish took refuge among their Pueblo neighbors at Taos. At Pecos, the Pueblos were forced to dig wells when it became too dangerous to walk the three miles to the river. In many areas, irrigated lands lay fallow, because it had become too dangerous for the men to tend to their crops, and hunger once again visited the Pueblo country. At Galisteo, the raiders made off with every single cow and horse, and the inhabitants were reduced to eating hides and toasted elk shoes. Within a decade the village would be a ghost town.

Despite their accommodation with the Spanish, by the last quarter of the 18th century the Pueblos were facing a calamity very similar in kind to that which they had known 100 years earlier. Wracked by famine, epidemic (smallpox ravaged the Pueblo country in 1780–81 and 1788–89), and ceaseless raids, the Pueblos found their already severely reduced numbers diminishing still further. Village after village suffered severe population decline or complete abandonment, until only 19 of the 66 Rio Grande pueblos first described by the Spaniards remained. The 20 former pueblos of the southern Tiwas, for exam-

Spectators await the beginning of a Snake Dance at the Hopi villages in 1896. Over the years, outsiders have spun various lurid fantasies about the role of rattlesnakes in the Pueblo religion.

ple, had been combined into one (Isleta), while the 11 villages of Jemez now comprised a single community.

Once again, the Pueblos survived, sustained by their traditional ways and beliefs and their identity as a people. After a series of military victories, made possible in large part by the help of their Pueblo allies, the Spanish secured a truce with the hostile tribes, and slowly the Pueblos began to recover. They had gained prestige in their defense of the province and earned an secure place within New Mexican society. Working relationships had emerged between the Pueblos and the Spanish, and out of mutual need and suffering had been born mutual respect, tolerance, and cooperation. The century had proven to be a cycle of trial and restoration, and the time-honored ways of the Pueblos—ways of planting, ways of praying and dancing, ways of fighting—had successfully met each challenge. ▲

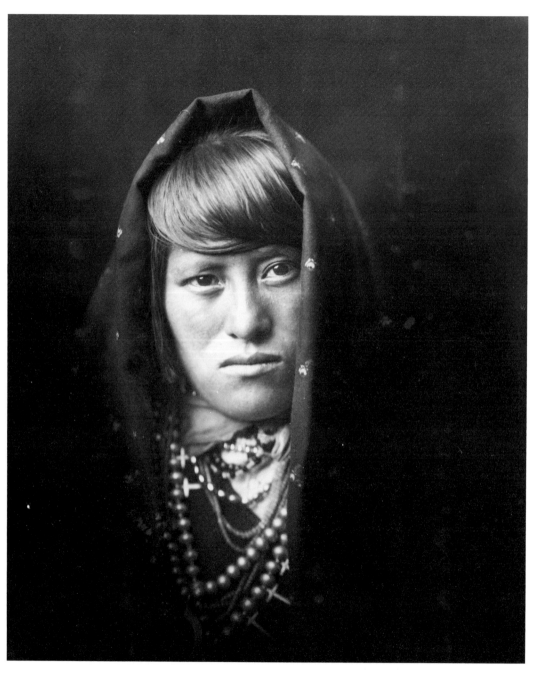

Juana, an Acoma pueblo woman photographed by Edward S. Curtis in 1904. Many Pueblos bear Spanish first and last names.

UNDER
THE
MEXICANS

In the first decades of the 19th century, the Pueblos benefited from what might be termed a policy of benign neglect on the part of Spain's government, which was, for the most part, too preoccupied with political events in Europe to concern itself overmuch with New Mexico or the affairs of the Indians. By 1812, for example, there were just 22 Spanish missionaries in New Mexico, ostensibly responsible for 26 pueblos and 102 Spanish settlements, and there had not been a bishop in the colony for 50 years. The result, of course, was a further diminishing of the importance of the missions and a consequent flourishing of the traditional ceremonial life of the Pueblos.

The Pueblos also enjoyed a respite from Spanish involvement in their civil matters as well, as Spain grew unable or unwilling to commit military resources to the northernmost outposts of its American empire. In 1812, Spain committed only 121 soldiers to defend its

populace of 40,000 in New Mexico, where, though the Comanches remained at peace, raids by hostile Indians—primarily the Apaches—continued to such an extent that a government official lamented that "the people are now compelled, I should say reduced, to the necessity of organizing themselves into bands in order to harvest the crops."

New Mexico was threatened not just by the Apaches but by the territorial ambitions of the new republic of the United States. The Louisiana Purchase expanded the borders of the United States beyond the Mississippi to those of New Mexico, and in 1806 a lieutenant in the U.S. army, Zebulon Pike, was found with a contingent of soldiers wandering about Spanish territory on some mysterious mission. Pedro Bautista Pino, a colonial official, was just one of the Spaniards in New Mexico who was aware of the danger posed by the United States to Spain's interests there, as he

Coiled baskets from Zia pueblo. With manufactured goods difficult to come by in New Mexico, Spanish settlers came to rely on Indian goods.

advised his government in 1812: "The purchase of Louisiana by the United States has opened the way for the Americans to arm and incite the wild Indians against us; also the way is open for the Americans to invade the province. Once this territory is lost, it will be impossible to recover it."

In this climate, the Spanish in New Mexico became even more dependent on the goodwill of the Pueblos. Trade with the Comanches remained a vital component of the New Mexican economy, and many of the *comancheros*—as those traders willing to venture out onto the plains to barter items such as bread, flour, cornmeal, sugar candy, dried pumpkins, onions, tobacco, and iron arrow and lance points with the Comanches for horses, mules, buffalo robes, and meat were known—were often Pueblo entrepreneurs. Though regarded as somewhat unsavory for their willingness to provide a past and potentially future enemy with guns and ammunition, the comancheros were nevertheless held to be important members of the Pueblo economy for their role in keeping the peace.

By this point, the Pueblos were being championed by the Spanish as paragons of "civilization" in contrast to the "savage" Apaches. "The Apache tribe is the most obnoxious and cruel of all," Pino wrote. "They always go naked, they kill and rob most treacherously; they torture their prisoners in the most cruel manner, often scalping them alive; then they cut up the bodies into small pieces." But Pueblo villages, wrote Pino, were wor-

thy of comparison with the cities of Spain, and their inhabitants equally graceful and clean: "Even the houses of the Indians consist of three, four, or even six stories. Anyone who has seen the homes in Cadíz (with the exception of the *rejas* and balconies) has seen the equivalent of these. All the people wear clothes and shoes. The women (to whom nature has granted grace and beauty) wear tunics and mantillas, and cut their hair, as had been customary from remote antiquity, and as do our gypsies today."

With the privilege of being "civilized," however, came both the rights and responsibilities of Spanish citizenship as determined by Spanish law. The Spanish government proclaimed the legal equality of Spaniards and Indians on February 9, 1811, and Spanish officials were quick to seize upon this change in the status of New Mexico's Indians in their recommendations regarding land reform. This was the initial volley in a battle that would haunt the Pueblos for years to come.

Previously, the communal "Pueblo league"—approximately 2.6 square miles measured from the cross of each pueblos' cemetery and extending in the four cardinal directions—had been Indian land whose inviolability had been sanctioned by the crown. Now, Pino and other officials began to argue that because of the long decline in the Pueblo population (which he blamed solely on the supposed preference of Pueblo women for smaller families!), the leagues were too large to be needed or advantageously used by the Pueblo villages and should thus be opened up for Spanish settlement. Accordingly, in 1812 and 1813 new legal provisions were introduced that allowed up to half of Indian communal lands to be converted to private ownership by the Spanish. The result, particularly once New Mexico fell under the jurisdiction of the independent nation of Mexico, which obtained its freedom from Spain in 1821, was unauthorized encroachment upon Pueblo leagues and the filing by non-Indians of a number of formal petitions requesting titles to communally held Pueblo property.

Though the Mexican law regarding land ownership proved not always beneficial to the Pueblos, the Mexican neglect of the Spanish missionary system helped strengthen the Pueblo religion. The liberal spirit that inspired Mexico's independence movement was often anticlerical, and after independence the Mexican government showed little interest in rebuilding the mission system. By the 1830s, only five missionaries were assigned to the pueblos. According to a dispatch filed by a colonial official during that decade,

> Spiritual administration in New Mexico is in a truly doleful condition. Nothing is more common than to see an infinite number of the sick die without confession or extreme unction. It is indeed unusual to see the eucharist administered to the sick. Corpses remain unburied for many days, and children are baptized at the cost of a thousand hardships. A

great many unfortunate people spend most of the Sundays in the year without hearing mass. Churches are in a state of near ruin, and most of them are unworthy of being called the temple of God.

By contrast, the same author reported the kivas to be in good repair and native religion to be flourishing:

> All of the pueblos have their *estufas*. This is the name the Indians give to the subterranean rooms that have only one door. There they gather to practice their dances, to celebrate their feasts, and to have their meetings. These estufas are like impenetrable temples, where they gather to discuss mysteriously their misfortunes or good fortunes, their happiness or grief. The doors of the estufas are always closed to us, the Spaniards, as they call us.

The civil and ecclesiastical neglect of the New Mexico province that characterized the Mexican administration was welcomed by the Pueblos, who were now free to openly pursue the rich ceremonial life and ways of being that had secretly sustained them through the long years of persecution and oppression. Non-Indian observers were impressed by the order of the Pueblo communities and the tenacity of their inhabitants, whose architecture, arts, dress, foods, and other customs seemed impervious to external political upheaval and social change. Pueblo residents wore the clothing of their ancestors, for the most part

The opening of the Santa Fe Trail in 1822 brought an extensive American influence to the Pueblo country for the first time. The trail connected Santa Fe, New Mexico, with Independence, Missouri.

(as described below by the American observer Josiah Gregg), and lived in homes not unlike those found by the Spaniards of the entrada three centuries earlier (as described below by the Spaniard Antonio Barreiro):

> The dress of many of the Pueblos has become assimilated in some respects to that of the common Mexicans; but by far the greatest portion still retain most of their aboriginal costume. The Tadsas and others of the north somewhat resemble the prairie tribes in this respect; but the Pueblos to the south and west of Santa Fe dress in a different style, which is said to be similar in many respects to that of the aboriginal inhabitants of the city of Mexico. . . . They mostly wear a kind of short breeches and long stockings, the use of which they most probably acquired from the Spaniards. The *saco*, a species of woolen jacket without sleeves, completes their exterior garment; except during inclement seasons, when they make use of the tilma. Very few of them have hats or headdress of any kind; and they generally wear their hair long— commonly fashioned into a queue, wrapped with some colored stuff. The squaws of the northern tribes dress pretty much like those of the Prairies; but the usual costume of the females of the southern and western Pueblos is a handsome kind of small blanket of dark color, which is drawn under one arm and tacked over the other shoulder, leaving both arms free and naked. It is generally worn with a cotton chemise underneath and is bound about the waist with a girdle. We rarely if ever see a thoroughbred Pueblo woman in Mexican dress.

> The pueblos mentioned have a truly remarkable construction— they have well-protected walls and are two or more stories high. The lower floors, which are generally called *cois*, are completely enclosed, and in the ceiling, between the vigas, are small doors with ladders which lead to the rooms above. The upper floors have corridors and balconies of wood, which always face inside toward the plaza of the pueblo. This presents a well-organized system of defense in case of attacks by the wild Indians who surround New Mexico.

In addition to farming and some herding, buffalo hunts were conducted by the Pueblos in June and October, utilizing specially trained horses, with an estimated 10,000 to 12,000 head killed annually. The hides of the winter kills were highly prized, both for individual use and as a trade commodity, while in the spring the animals were taken for the meat alone. The Pueblos also continued to hunt eagles in their traditional manner, with the object of capturing the majestic birds alive. Eagle feathers were among the most highly prized trade commodities, valued both as decorative elements for clothing and for use on arrows. Perhaps because of the eagle's prowess as a flyer and hunter, arrows

An 1897 ceremonial dance at the Mishongnovi pueblo of the Hopis. Because of their more remote location, the Hopis were the most successful of the Pueblo peoples in resisting Spanish influence.

adorned with eagle feathers were greatly valued—eagle feathers were said to possess a special ability to cut the air—and could be traded to the Apaches and other tribes for horses. Most pueblos kept several captive eagles.

Isolation and neglect by the Mexican government also strengthened the cooperative bonds forged between the Pueblo and rural Hispanic communities.

The two groups frequently worked together to maintain and regulate the use of irrigation ditches. Hispanic families were welcomed visitors at feast days and Pueblo dancers performed in Santa Fe in full regalia at the annual independence day celebrations.

In their struggle for self-sufficiency, the Hispanic population gradually adopted many elements of the Pueblo

With their peaceful, permanent villages and sedentary, agricultural way of life, the Pueblos seemed to many non-Indians the least "savage" of the Native American peoples.

way of life. Pino reported in 1812, for example, on the settlers' reliance on Native American medicines: "There are many medicinal herbs of extraordinary value for curing all kinds of diseases. The sedentary Indians [the Pueblos], as well as the wild Indians [Comanches, Apaches, et al.] know these herbs well and use them to great advantage. These are the only medicinal means available—thanks be to providence for them—since there is not one single medicinal dispensary in the entire province, and only one physician."

The diet of Spanish settlers was also largely adopted from the Pueblos, with tortillas, atole, pinole, chile, and frijoles constituting staples for both groups. Hispanics in New Mexico often used Pueblo pottery to prepare such food in, and Pueblo wicker ware, so tightly woven that it was waterproof, was valued for its convenience to travelers.

The Mexican government's inability, or disinclination, to protect the most remote regions of its territories provided yet another reason for the drawing together of Pueblos and Hispanics. Over time, the peace secured by Juan Bautista de Anza in 1786 broke down, and attacks by the Navajos, Apaches, and Utes increased in frequency until the New Mexico settlements began to feel as beleaguered as before the Comanche peace. Joint Pueblo and Mexican retaliatory expeditions were again organized to counter the onslaught. For the most part, the Pueblo units were essentially autonomous and answered to their own elected war leaders.

The cultural exchange between Pueblos and Hispanics that characterized this period was limited to the eastern settlements, however. Geographical isolation, their own inclinations, and Apache and Navajo raids combined to ensure that neither the Hopis nor the Zunis exhibited any significant Spanish cultural influence throughout the Mexican period. With the exception of fur trappers and the occasional American military expedition, few outsiders visited the Zuni or Hopi lands.

Although epidemics of typhoid and smallpox killed almost 10 percent of the Pueblo population between 1837 and 1840, the first decades of the 19th century proved to be the least calamitous for the Pueblo of any period since the coming of the Spanish, and there seemed little basis for José Agustín de Escudero's 1849 assertion that the "Indian race is vanishing." The Pueblos had succeeded in preserving their cultural identity and political autonomy while simultaneously attaining a position of legal equality; the Pueblos had not only maintained the integrity of their own traditions, but, through their various contributions, were helping to create a distinctly New Mexican culture. Indeed, much of the unique character of the New Mexican territory that would so startle the Americans upon their entry had been derived from Pueblo ways of being and living that would *not* die—ways that were inseparable from the land and survival upon it. ▲

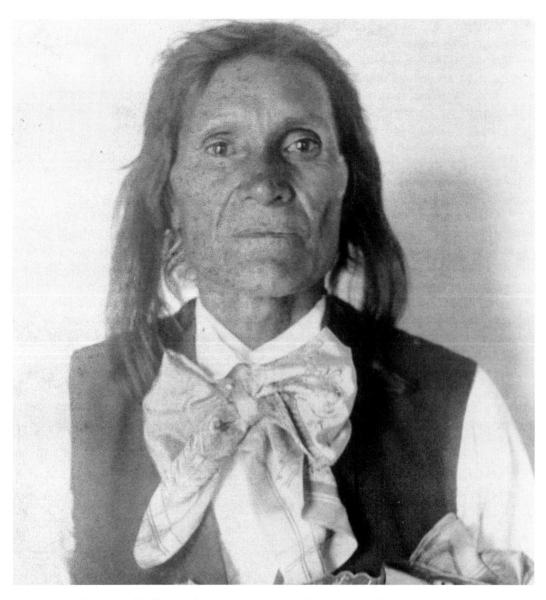

Francisco Vigil was the governor of San Ildefonso pueblo in 1900.
The Pueblos adopted the title of governor from the Spanish and
adapted it to their own system of government. In most pueblos today,
the governor is still, as he has been since the days of the Spanish,
appointed by the cacique, or tribal leader; in others he is elected by
popular ballot. The governor is responsible, in Joe S. Sando's
words, "for all tribal business with the modern world."

THE
AMERICANS
COME

A new era began for the Pueblos on August 13, 1846. That evening, as the sun was setting, a new flag was hoisted over the governor's palace in Santa Fe. To the roar of a 13-gun salute sounded by artillery stationed high above the city, an American force led by Stephen Watts Kearny took possession of New Mexico, which the Mexicans relinquished without firing a shot.

The following morning Pueblo leaders arrived in the capital to pledge their allegiance to the new regime and gauge what the transition would mean for them. The Americans were promptly invited to visit the pueblo of Santo Domingo, where they were treated to a festive display of showmanship intended to dramatically convey the community's self-proclaimed sovereignty and strength as a people, as Lieutenant William H. Emory, one of the foremost American explorers of the Southwest, described at great length:

This has been a great day. An invitation was received, some days since, from the Pueblo Indians to visit their town of Santo Domingo. From height to height, as we advanced, we saw horsemen disappearing at full speed. As we arrived abreast of the town we were shown by a guide, posted there for the purpose, the road to Santo Domingo. The chief part of the command and the wagon train were sent along the highway; the general [Kearny] with his staff and Captain Burgwyn's squadron of dragoons, wended his way along the bridle path nearly due west to the town. We had not proceeded far, before we met ten or fifteen sachemic looking old Indians, well mounted, and two of them carrying gold-headed canes with tassels, the emblems of office in New Mexico.

Salutations over, we jogged along, and, in the course of conversation, the alcalde, a grave and majestic old Indian, said, as if casually, "We shall meet some Indians presently, mounted, and dressed for war, but they are the young men of my town, friends come to receive you, and I wish you to caution your men not to fire upon them when they ride towards them."

When within few miles of the town, we saw a cloud of dust rapidly advancing, and soon the air was rent with a terrible yell, resembling the Florida war-whoop. The first object that caught my eye through the column of dust, was a fierce pair of buffalo horns, overlapped with long shaggy hair. As they approached, the sturdy form of a naked Indian revealed itself beneath the horns, with shield and lance, dashing at full speed, on a white horse, which, like his own body, was painted all the colors of the rainbow; and then, one by one, his followers came on, painted to the eyes, their own heads and their horses covered with all the strange equipments that the brute creation could afford in the way of horns, skulls, tails, feathers, and claws.

As they passed us, one rank on each side, they fired a volley under our horses' bellies from the right and from the left. Our well-trained dragoons sat motionless on their horses, which went along without pricking an ear or showing any sign of excitement.

Arrived in the rear, the Indians circled round, dropped into a walk on our flanks until their horses recovered breath, when off they went at full speed, passing to our front, and when there, the opposite files met, and each man selected his adversary and kept up a running fight, with muskets, lances, and bows and arrows. Sometimes a fellow would stoop almost to the earth to shoot under his horse's belly, at full speed, or to shield himself from an impending blow. So they continued to pass and repass us all the way to the steep cliff which overhangs the town. There they filed on each side of the road, which descends through a deep canon, and halted on the peaks of the cliffs. Their motionless forms projected against the clear blue sky above, formed studies for an artist.

Questions regarding the exact legal status of the Pueblos within the jurisdiction of the United States were, however, to plague Anglo-Pueblo relations for years to come. American Indian policy consisted essentially of a plan of isolation, whereby the expansion of western settlement would be facilitated through the establishment of reservations. Such a position allowed for limited or no political participation on the part of the native groups concerned, as the historian Edward Spicer has explained:

The assumption was that the United States had acquired the whole territory and that Anglos were free to settle where they wished and to pass through the territory, and hence that Indian land rights were not recognized. This curious paradox—recognition by the Anglos of the Indians as a political unit capable of making binding treaties but without rights in the land where they lived—

Brigadier General Stephen Watts Kearny conquered New Mexico for the United States in 1846. The Territorial Assembly established by Kearny recognized the rights of the Pueblos "to resist encroachment, claim, or trespass" upon their lands.

provided no basis whatever for mutual adjustment of interests; it constituted a sort of reversal of the Spanish policy which recognized the land rights of the Indians but not their political independence of Spain.

Indeed, the arrival of the Americans posed a much different set of challenges for the Pueblos than those they had faced when New Mexico was nominally a Spanish or Mexican possession, as the Pueblo historian Joe S. Sando has pointed out. "For more than 125 years," Sando writes, "[the Pueblos] would contend with cultural and political conflicts that would have drained the energies of any people. There was no question now of fighting the intruders and successfully evicting them from Indian land, as the Indian revolutionaries of 1680 had done. Nor was it possible to effect an alliance in the way of the Spanish at the opening of the 18th century, providing some type of peaceful co-existence between the people of the Pueblos and the Anglos. Of understanding there was none. Of misconception and error in judgment there was a vast quantity. . . . The United States laid a heavy hand on Pueblo life, religion, and culture."

The self-sufficiency of the Pueblos and their settled, agricultural way of life posed a paradox for American policy-makers. Early legislation recognized the Pueblos' standing as citizens and claims to their land (although the Indians were denied the right to vote except in elections to determine officials in the pueblos themselves), and American officials in New Mexico were quick to point out the contrasts between such "savage" tribes as the Apaches, Utes, Navajos, Comanches, Cayugas, Cheyennes, and Arapahos, and the "civilized" Pueblos. The first U.S. Indian agent in New Mexico, James Calhoun, was equally quick to recognize that removal of the Pueblos to one large, consolidated reservation was unthinkable and that the Pueblos represented a vital and integrated component of the New Mexican economy:

> To remove and consolidate the Indians of the Various Pueblos at a common point, is out of the question—the general character of their houses, are superior to those of Santa Fe—they have rich valleys to cultivate—grow quantities of corn and wheat, and raise vast herds of horses, mules, sheep and goats—all of which, may be immensely increased by properly stimulating their industry, and instructing them in agricultural arts—for the reasons, in an economical point of view, heretofore given, the Government of the United States should instruct these people in their agricultural pursuits—they are a valuable, and *available* people, and as firmly fixed in their homes, as anyone can be in the United States.
>
> Their lands are held by Spanish and Mexican grants—to what extent is unknown—and in their religion they are Catholics, with a certain admixture of an early superstition, with its ceremonials; all of which attaches them to the soil of their fathers—the soil upon which they

The arrival of American settlers in New Mexico in large numbers brought a new outside influence to bear on the Pueblos. This picture was taken in Santa Fe in 1880; note that many of the buildings in the background are not dissimilar in construction to those of the Pueblos.

came into existence, and the soil upon which they have been reared—and their concentration is not advisable.

But the Pueblos' self-sufficiency left them excluded from certain legal protections—dubious as these may have been in practice—enjoyed by other tribes under U.S. jurisdiction, such as laws preventing trespass on and acquisition of tribal lands. Whereas such laws "had been made for wandering savages," a U.S. judge ruled in 1869, "the Pueblos" had been "living for three centuries in fenced abodes and cultivating the soil for the maintenance of themselves and their families and giving an example by their virtue, honesty, and industry to their more civilized neighbors." The same judge went on to point out that "the court has known the conduct and habits of these people for 18 or 20 years, and we say, without fear of successful contradiction, that you may pick out 1,000 of the best Americans in New Mexico, and 1,000 of the worst Pueblo Indians, and there will be found less, vastly less, murder, robbery, theft, or other crimes among a thousand of the worst Pueblo Indians than among a thousand of the best Mexicans or Americans in New Mexico."

But virtue offered the Pueblos no legal protection against encroachment on their lands by the rapidly expanding Hispanic and American population of

New Mexico. Lands to which the Pueblos had no legal title, but which they had long used for agriculture or grazing, were claimed by settlers, and existing Pueblo land grants continued to be inadequate to support the growing Indian population. Disputes over land became frequent; some of the most serious took place at San Juan, Santa Anna, Laguna, and Acoma. In some locations, unscrupulous traders and merchants opened unwanted businesses on Pueblo lands, corrupting the Indian population through the sale of alcohol and the introduction of gambling.

As might be expected in an essentially arid region, increased population meant increased competition for water rights. New Mexico state and municipal archives from the 19th century are rife with accounts of water-rights disputes, many of them involving Pueblos. In addition, as the population of New Mexico grew, increasingly extensive ranching and logging operations began to claim many of the natural resources on which the Pueblos depended. Within a short time after the conclusion of the Civil War, for example, American settlers had populated almost every acre suitable for grazing with sheep or cattle, and many regions in or near the Rio Grande valley were quickly overgrazed. Logging companies stripped the mountains of much of their timber, causing much heavier runoff from the rains and the spring melt, which resulted in devastating flooding of the Pueblo lands along the Rio Grande and its tributaries.

Even Americans who did not neces-

This 1850 lithograph of Hos-ta, the governor of Jemez pueblo, illustrated the published edition of the journal of Lieutenant Richard Simpson, a U.S. military officer stationed in New Mexico soon after its conquest by the Americans.

sarily intend to settle in New Mexico left their mark on the pueblos. Calhoun reported numerous flagrant frauds, trespasses, and other abuses perpetrated on the Indians by pioneers destined for points farther west, such as the gold fields of California. A favorite scam of American travelers was to impersonate government officials and requisition livestock and other supplies from a particular pueblo with the promise of forth-coming government restitution. Zuni was especially hard hit, as it was situated on a number of important trade routes, and the pueblo suffered frequent losses of livestock and damage to its fields, as one appalled fellow American wayfarer reported:

> What is shockingly discreditable to the American name, emigrants commit the grossest wrongs against those excellent Indians by taking, in the name of the United States, such horses, mules, and sheep, and grain as they desire, carefully concealing their true name, but assuming official authority and bearing. A wrong of this kind had been perpetrated a few days previous to our arrival there.

Remarkably, such mistreatment did not dampen Pueblo hospitality; Calhoun reported "a hearty reception" upon his visit to Zuni, where the Indians wel-comed him "in the most uproarious, wild, and indescribable manner, offer-ing to us large quantities of fruit and bread; all of which was becomingly received."

The Pueblos had other causes for dis-content with the Americans. Despite promises of protection from the ravages of the nomadic tribes, Pueblo communi-ties continued to be assaulted, but the Americans, unlike the Spanish and Mex-icans, sought to prevent them from retal-iating. They urged the Pueblos to leave the responsibility for defending their community in the hands of the U.S.

Army, which by 1855 was stationed at six different forts in or near Pueblo coun-try, but the Pueblos found the army's protection inadequate. Pueblo auxiliary forces were called upon much less often, and when they were used they were often not compensated satisfactorily.

Pueblo leaders repeatedly requested munitions and permission to use them from Calhoun in Santa Fe, who for-warded their pleas to Washington to no avail. The governor of Jemez reported daily altercations with Navajos, at Coch-iti Apaches swooped down from the mountains with regularity, killing men, taking women and children captive, and stealing animals, and at Zuni residents carried arms wherever they went and guarded all livestock 24 hours a day. At the latter pueblo there were 555 men of fighting age in 1850, but only 32 guns and limited ammunition.

The Hopis, who were even more iso-lated from the eastern settlements than the Zuni, found themselves exception-ally hard pressed by the surrounding Navajos. By 1846, the Hopi population had dwindled to an estimated 2,450, while the surrounding Navajos num-bered anywhere between 7,000 and 14,000. When the thriving Navajos began to push onto lands the Hopis tra-ditionally held as their own, the Hopi villages sent a delegation to Santa Fe in 1850 and again in 1851 to try and obtain assistance. Though a number of govern-ment surveyors and various other offi-cials were dispatched to the Hopi villages during the next two decades, aid was not forthcoming; in the 1860s drought and a smallpox epidemic made their situation even more desperate. Many Hopi families eventually sought refuge with the Zunis, resulting in an interchange of cultural traits between these already closely related Pueblo peoples.

At the same time that American military officials were refusing Pueblo requests to defend their homes, they worried about the Pueblos "conspiring" with the "wild Indians." Pueblo Indians continued to trade with the Comanches and venture out on the plains to visit and hunt buffalo with various plains tribes until about 1880. In the 1850s, Lieutenant Amiel W. Whipple of the U.S. Army reported finding Pueblo traders from Santo Domingo as far east as Oklahoma. Unregulated Pueblo contact with the "hostiles" was a source of great consternation to those engaged in the enterprise of subduing the likes of the Comanches, Kiowas, Cheyennes, and Arapahos.

Though soldiers, traders, and government officials constantly blustered about putting a stop to such contact, the Great Plains trade did not seriously diminish until the plains tribes began to be confined to reservations and the buffalo population was virtually eliminated by American hunters. The Pueblo peoples suffered as well from a dimunition of game animals in their territories after the onset of large-scale American settlement. In 1867, Antonio Joseph Martinez, a priest at Taos, reported the devastating effects for Pueblo hunters and predicted even more drastic consequences:

Now they encounter the same difficulties, but stay away four or five months, and not only return exhausted, after traveling over vast extent of ground, but even without their horses, and frequently without anything at all. This is further affirmed by the settlers residing in the different parts of the north, who bring with them a great quantity of all sorts of articles to exchange for buffaloes, and thus form a traffic very beneficial in various ways to the Indians, obliging them to extend the hunt for the animals for a greater return, in order to sustain themselves, and to obtain the articles sold by the traders. Urged by this necessity, there is no such limitation to the destruction of the buffaloes as is observed by the economy of the different nations, which at certain periods forbid and limit the hunting season; in this manner protecting these animals, and the most precious, which are breeding in the spring, though the latter are not even spared, and thus causes the loss of millions of calves. It is easily imagined that an attack made upon a herd of buffalo cows, amounting to three or four thousand, the most part of them with calves, running away to a distance of fifty or sixty leagues, must naturally cause a great loss, if not of the totality, at least of the greatest part of the young ones, as it is proved by experience. It is certain that the buffaloes must greatly diminish in consequence and that this constant slaughter will finally result in the extinction of the species in a very short time.

Three Zuni men, photographed in approximately 1880. The American presence in the Pueblo country posed a new challenge to the traditional way of life of the Indians there.

Pueblo Indians use horses to thresh wheat; a late 19th-century etching. The Navajos often lent the Pueblos their horses for threshing in exchange for payment in wheat.

But if subsistence by hunting was becoming more and more difficult, advances in agricultural technology were lightening the burden of Pueblo cultivators. Indian agents, called farmers, had been assigned to each Pueblo community, save Hopi, by 1869. Their chief duty was to provide agricultural assistance, and although the kind of crops the Pueblos grew and the techniques the Indians used to tend them did not greatly change, the Pueblos quickly adopted the latest tools the American agents introduced: plows, shovels, hoes, rakes, pitchforks, and spring wagons. By the 1870s, government funds were made available to the Pueblos for the construction of dams and wells and the improvement of irrigation ditches. Despite these improvements, however, many time-honored Pueblo agricultural practices continued. In 1846, Lieutenant Emory described a long-standing Pueblo method of winnowing wheat, "which is done by making a circular 'corral' on a level ground of clay; upon this floor they scatter the wheat, turn in a dozen or more mules, and one or two Indians, who, with whoops, yells, and blows, keep the affrighted brutes constantly in motion. To separate the wheat from the chaff, both Indians and Mexicans use a simple hand-barrow, with a bottom of raw bull's hide perforated with holes. I should suppose it must take an hour to winnow a bushel."

New agricultural tools represented only one category of the many and varied American goods that had been making their way to Pueblo country since the opening of the Santa Fe Trail in 1822. One hundred wagons strong, the caravans usually arrived in July and were met by eager buyers from as far away as the Texas settlement of El Paso and the Mexican province of Sonora. With the availability of cheaply produced cotton and woolen cloth, metal crockery, and china vessels, certain Pueblo crafts—notably pottery and weaving—suffered a decline in productivity. The weaving of ceremonial items, such as belts and sashes, continued in the Rio Grande pueblos, and the more isolated Hopis did not experience any disruption in their textile arts, though pottery making was nearly abandoned. The Pueblos abandoned weaving for another reason as well: as woven cloth and blankets had been among the items most commonly

Acoma pueblo at the beginning of the 20th century.

An old Pueblo house. "This is the time of the great question," a delegation of Pueblos wrote in the early 20th century. "Shall we peacefully but strongly and deathlessly hold to the religion of our fathers, to our own religion. . . . There is no future for the race of the Indians if its religion is killed."

demanded by the Spanish as tribute, the Pueblos had long associated such handicrafts with Spanish oppression, making their production perhaps more easy to abandon.

Another trade item that began to make its appearance in Pueblo homes by the late 1870s was window glass. Previously, the Pueblos had covered windows with small panels of mica. Slowly, windows and doors (often of milled lumber and iron) were added to ground-floor rooms, and ladders and upper-story homes began to disappear. As raids by other Indians began to cease in the 1870s, Pueblo families moved closer to their fields, creating small satellite villages away from the main pueblo compound.

Changes in material culture were certainly more visible under the new American regime than were changes in Pueblo spiritual life. For the most part, the U.S. authorities in New Mexico were more interested, as regarded the Pueblos, in economics and education than in religious conversion. Although Jean Lamy was installed in 1851 as New Mexico's first resident bishop, his arrival did not signal a renewed interest in the Pueblos on the part of the Catholic church, which during his time in New Mexico concentrated its efforts in urban areas and on meeting the needs of its non-Indian members. Though Bishop Lamy was responsible for the construction of 45 new churches and several schools, by the end of the century only two day schools and two boarding schools existed for Indian students.

Protestant missionaries took advantage of the apathy of their Catholic counterparts to attempt to establish a foothold in the pueblos. A Baptist mission and school was established in 1851 at Laguna but was abandoned soon afterwards. Presbyterian minister John Menaul, who printed his own reader in English and the Keresan language, enjoyed somewhat greater success with the mission he established at the same pueblo in 1875, and two years later the Presbyterians expanded to Zuni, where they built a mission and school. Similar efforts were made at Isleta and Jemez. Mormon Jacob Hamblin took a special interest in the Hopis and tried for six years to convert them to his faith, even taking a group to the Mormon settlements in Utah, but in the end his labors were fruitless. In 1870, a Moravian mission was built at Oraibi, followed by Mormon and Baptist missions at Moenkopi and Oraibi five years later.

Though few overt attempts to suppress the Pueblo native religion were made by the Americans, the Indians, conditioned to secrecy by years of Spanish suppression, continued for the most part to conduct their religious ceremonies as private rituals held away from the eyes of outsiders. To this day, the Pueblos are cautious about allowing outsiders to witness their ceremonies; although some villages allow tourists to view their dances, most discourage photographers from taking pictures of such ceremonies.

Although a number of issues affecting them remained unresolved—questions of legal status, political autonomy, land and water rights, and religious freedom—by the 1870s the Pueblos stood ready to enter the modern era (symbolized most dramatically by the coming of the railroad to Pueblo country) with their tribal identity intact. Through adaptation, assimilation, and compartmentalization, the Pueblos had succeeded in maintaining their unity as a people over the course of more than three centuries of outside invasion, settlement, and related cultural subversion. Despite continued challenges to their way of life and the various problems inherent in their relationship with the U.S. government, the Pueblo, in the last decades of the 19th century, had little reason to fear either permanent exile from their traditional homeland or cultural extinction—in which regard they were much more fortunate than the vast majority of other Native American peoples. Nevertheless, the cultural integrity that had served them so well in the face of such affronts would be newly and greatly tested in the decades to come. ▲

A Pueblo woman carries wood at the village of Cochiti. With very little industry or development, most pueblos today are economically depressed, and the unemployment rate at some approaches 80 percent in winter.

TOWARD
THE
FUTURE

In the last decades of the 19th century, land claims and water rights continued to be the two most important issues affecting the Pueblos, whose legal status under U.S. law remained ambiguous. Denied the full legal rights and privileges of U.S. citizens (such as the right to vote), by virtue of new court rulings the Pueblos were also again denied, because of their "civilized" status, the protection of laws intended to otherwise safeguard Indian lands. Arable land in New Mexico was scarce, and as the rate of non-Indian settlement increased as the 19th century came to an end, the Pueblos found their landholdings significantly reduced.

At the same time that the Pueblos found themselves and their homeland increasingly endangered, outside interest in their ancient and contemporary ways of life was growing. Between 1876 and 1904, a number of fairs and expositions featured displays of Indian arti-

facts and lifestyles; some of these displays even showed live Indians at work. For example, a popular exhibit in the Anthropological Building at the World's Columbian Exposition in 1893 showed several Indian groups, including Pueblos, engaged in traditional activities. The fair's exhibits also included a model Indian school as a representation of the "civilized" future of the Indians. At the Louisiana Purchase Exposition of 1904, the Indian Building exhibit featured a model school with Indian students on one side of the hallway and booths of Indians demonstrating traditional crafts on the other side. Pueblos were included in the portrayal of different Indian lifestyles; their presence, according to historian Robert A. Trennert, was intended to reinforce "the already developing image of the southwestern Indians as a peaceful, charming, and artistic group of people whose culture might warrant preservation." To many Americans, the historian Richard H. Frost wrote, the Pueblos were emerging as "the most interesting of the American tribes," a fascinating mixture of "civilized ways," in the form of their agricultural practices and sedentary way of life, and traditional religious beliefs and rituals.

The Indian exhibits were exceedingly popular attractions that helped promote the Southwest as a tourist attraction, a notion that had first become prevalent with the extension of the Southern Pacific and Arizona railroads to New Mexico and Arizona in 1880. For the first time, the Southwest was easily accessible to easterners. At the same time, interest in the region was being piqued by explorers' narratives, which were very popular with eastern readers; magazine articles, the paintings of various western artists, and the pictures taken by photographers, such as John K. Hillers, Timothy O'Sullivan, and William Henry Jackson, who worked with the various topographical surveys of the region sponsored by the federal government after the Civil War.

Tourism came as a mixed blessing to the Pueblos, providing them with a much needed source of income but also imposing upon their privacy. One positive consequence of this new interest by outsiders in the Pueblo Country was a resurgence of interest in Pueblo traditional crafts, as the Indians discovered that tourists would pay good money for authentic Indian artifacts. The sale of pottery, jewelry, and paintings became an important aspect of the Pueblo econ-omy, and several Pueblo artists—most notably Maria and Julian Martinez, their son Popovi Da, Antonita Roybal, Ramona Gonzales, and Maximiliana Martinez—won international renown for their pottery.

Among the new visitors to the Pueblo Country at this time were anthropologists and archaeologists eager to study a living though still traditional Indian culture. The ethnologist Frank Hamilton Cushing, for example, lived among the Zuni from 1879 to 1884, and the pioneering archaeologist-historian Adolph Bandolier stayed briefly at Santo Domingo before moving to Cochiti. Though some of these scholars gained acceptance by learning the language and adopting the style of dress of the particular pueblo they were studying, the Pueblos generally regarded such visitors with distrust. The primary reason for such suspicion was the Pueblos' justified belief that these outsiders wished to publish detailed information about their religious rites, information that the Indians regarded as sacred and guarded as a secret. The Indians often responded to prying professors by putting on their credulous guests, such as when the Tewas told anthropologist Matilda Coxe Stevenson "that human sacrifice was practiced in at least two of the villages." There were, however, positive consequences of the scholars' interest. Pueblo men were often employed as laborers on archaeological digs, and various scholarly discoveries stimulated an interest in Pueblo history and culture and its preservation. The Museum of New Mexico,

Mishongnovi, one of the Hopi villages.

which houses a large collection of Pueblo material, was established in 1909 in large part as a result of such interest.

Filmmakers were another new type of visitor to the Pueblo country. In 1912, the legendary director D. W. Griffith and his film company came to Isleta, which was to be the setting for his newest movie, *A Pueblo Legend*, starring Mary Pickford. The pueblo elders, however, felt that Griffith's script did not portray them with sufficient dignity—the director admitted to taking artistic license with the costumes—and asked the company to leave. Griffith's offer of $2,000 was insufficient to make them change their minds, and he had to finish his filming in Albuquerque.

In other ways, the ongoing influx of non-Indian settlers caused more familiar problems. Disease continued to be a problem, with tuberculosis, smallpox, and trachoma, which causes blindness, exerting a particularly heavy toll. Though Pueblo distrust of modern medical practices—the Zuni, for instance, initially refused to be vaccinated for smallpox—aggravated the problem, for the most part the available health services for the Pueblos were grossly inadequate.

But as it would be for most Native American peoples in the early 20th century (and as it remains today), the question of land ownership remained the Pueblos' greatest problem, particularly

A Zuni girl photographed by Edward S. Curtis near the beginning of the 20th century.

as regarded water rights. By 1912, for example, San Juan had lost 75 percent of its irrigable acres and San Ildefonso had lost 80 percent, and there were approximately 12,000 non-Indians living on 3,000 claims on Pueblo land. The major consequence of such encroachment was that the Pueblos were no longer able to rely on subsistence agriculture, and they turned increasingly to tourism and wage labor to support themselves.

By the terms of the New Mexico Enabling Act of 1910, the Pueblos were at last brought under federal jurisdiction under terms similar to those of other Indian peoples. When the legality of the legislation was challenged, the U.S. Supreme Court ruled, in *United States v. Sandoval*, what was exceedingly obvious to all but U.S. lawmakers—"that the Pueblo Indians were indeed Indians by race, customs and therefore government."

The ruling created an uproar in New Mexico, for as a result all land sales since 1848 were declared invalid, and thousands of non-Indians suddenly found themselves squatting illegally on Pueblo lands. The issue of land title in New Mexico was further complicated by the fact that many of the original Spanish land grants were vague or now nonexistent. The result was new tension between Pueblos and non-Indians.

In 1922, Senator Holm Bursum of New Mexico attempted to resolve the dispute through the introduction of new legislation. The Pueblos regarded the bill, which would have confirmed all non-Indian claims of title held since 1910, as biased in favor of the settlers, and they united to stop it. A written appeal from the All Indian Pueblo Council, on which all the governors of the 19 pueblos sat, pointed out to Congress that many Pueblos had less than one-tenth of the irrigated land necessary to support themselves and stated clearly that although the Pueblos wanted their lands protected, they did not wish to become dependents of the federal government. What they wanted was enough protection under the law to allow them to maintain their traditions, their dignity, and their independence. A delegation of Pueblos, which included Pueblo Abeita,

Sotero Ortiz, Antonio Romaro, Martin Vigil, and others, even visited Washington, D.C., to address Congress on the proposed legislation.

Pueblo opposition helped ensure the defeat of the Bursum Bill, and in 1924, the Pueblo Lands Act was adopted instead to settle disputed claims. Under the Pueblo Lands Act, non-Indian settlers with land titles had to prove 20 years of continuous possession, indicated by land-tax payment receipts. Non-Indian settlers without titles had to prove 35 years of possession, indicated by land-tax payment receipts. The Pueblos were compensated for lost land and water, with the money used to purchase more land or to construct irrigation projects.

The debate over the Bursum Bill helped to crystallize Anglo-American opinion about the Pueblos. The majority constituted those who believed that the only way for the Indians to "progress" was to assimilate and emulate the non-Indian way of life. On the other hand were sympathetic whites, such as John Collier, who wrote several favorable articles about the Pueblos and believed that preserving Native American culture was important. (Collier would ultimately become the nation's commissioner of Indian Affairs.) But even well-meaning whites sometimes tended to view the Pueblos as romantic abstractions rather than flesh-and-blood individuals, Indians as they were depicted by whites at fairs, expositions, and in literature rather than as they existed in real life; their support often had as much to do with their own ideas and interests as it did with what was best for the Indians. (The first Southwest Indian Fair was held in 1922 in Santa Fe. The fair encouraged quality craftsmanship through juried competitions, exhibitions, and market opportunities. The first Inter-tribal Indian Ceremonial was also held in 1922. It took place just outside of Gallup, New Mexico. The Southwest Indian Fair, or the Indian Market as it came to be known later, and the Inter-tribal Indian Ceremonial both grew to become important annual events and major tourist attractions.) For instance, Collier viewed Pueblo society as some sort of utopia and felt that it could provide a model for the rest of American society. He believed that the Pueblos had found the perfect balance between individual and community identity, a balance that was lacking in urbanized, industrialized America. Although he did many things that benefited the Pueblos and other Indians, he sometimes overlooked the desires of the Pueblos themselves if they were not in accordance with his vision.

In the 1920s, those non-Indians who espoused assimilation for the Pueblos held the upper hand, and the result was a new wave of intolerance regarding the Pueblo religion. With the Bureau of Indian Affairs pushing for cultural assimilation in the hope that all Indians would take up farming and Christianity and otherwise blend into the mainstream of American society, traditional native religions and customs were seen as stumbling blocks to this goal. Indian children were given Christian religious training in school and encouraged to abandon traditional values. On February 24, 1923, Charles H. Burke, commissioner of Indian Affairs, wrote to the Pueblos and asked them to give up their dances and religious practices within a year. Though he requested that they do so voluntarily, he implied that he would employ other tactics if the Indians did not comply.

The All Indian Pueblo Council responded in writing on May 1, 1924. In a missive addressed to the people of the United States, the Pueblos complained that they were being denied the right of religious liberty, stated that they had no intention of abandoning their religion, and pointed out that the government was not abiding by various treaties and agreements that guaranteed religious

An archaeological excavation near Zuni pueblo in the 1890s. Though such digs often yielded invaluable information about Native American history, the non-Indian scholars who directed them were often insensitive to the Indians' concerns regarding burial grounds and the disposition of discovered material.

tolerance. When the government ignored this appeal and went on to attempt to suppress the religious activities of the Pueblos and other Indians, the Pueblos responded by becoming even more secretive in the practice of their religion. They held ceremonies within the kivas and on occasion would not allow non-Indians into the pueblos.

After Collier was appointed commissioner of Indian Affairs in 1933, his reforms of federal Indian policy resulted in improved conditions for the Pueblos. Collier insisted, for example, that a portion of the federal money earmarked for social programs under President Franklin Roosevelt's New Deal policy be allotted to Native Americans. In New Mexico, such spending resulted in Pueblo artists being commissioned to produce work for display in public buildings. Day schools were built in Pueblo country and money was spent on education, although in general funding remained inadequate to provide quality services. On the national level, Collier was instrumental in the adoption of the Indian Reorganization Act (IRA) in 1934, which protected Indian lands, expanded reservation territories (in some cases), and assisted the Indians in setting up tribal governments to operate like municipalities. The IRA encouraged Indian groups to become self-sufficient by providing credit for agricultural and industrial projects as well as funding for college and technical training; the IRA was intended as well to promote acceptance of Indian cultures and traditional Indian values.

But for all Collier's good intentions, the Pueblos did not find him or the IRA to be totally benevolent. The Pueblos objected to restructuring their internal systems of government, for instance. Whereas the IRA proposed that Native American groups adopt constitutions that would have separated religion and politics, the Pueblos preferred their old system, in which religious authority and political power were inextricably linked. The Pueblos were also annoyed that for all Collier's support of traditional Indian culture, he allowed Catholic and Protestant missionaries, whom the Pueblos regarded as agents of cultural dissolution, to work unhampered among them.

Despite such disagreements, the Pueblos generally regarded Collier, whose tenure of office was destined to be relatively short, as a friend. With the coming of World War II, and the U.S. government's shifting of all available resources to the war effort, Collier found it increasingly difficult to implement his programs, and he resigned his office in 1945.

World War II affected the Pueblos in other ways as well. Many served in the U.S. armed forces during the war, and those veterans who returned to the Pueblo country after the war often took advantage of the G. I. Bill to further their education or start businesses. Others turned to wage work as the movement away from subsistence agriculture toward a cash economy continued. An increasing number of Pueblos (not all of them returning veterans) began seeking higher education.

A Pueblo man from San Ildefonso. Like most Native American peoples, the Pueblo have great respect for the wisdom and experience of the old.

Following the war, the Pueblos were affected as well by renewed assimilationist sentiment. In the 1950s, as a wave of hysterical anticommunism swept the United States, some Americans objected to the communal nature of Pueblo society. Others complained about the tax-free status of Indian lands and charged that the Indians enjoyed benefits that the average citizen did not, conveniently overlooking the role the United States played in depriving the Pueblos of their land and economic base. Such critics also ignored the fact that the Pueblos were not granted full rights as U.S. citizens—specifically the right to vote—until 1948.

Such assimilationist sentiment spurred the passage, in 1952, of legislation intended to terminate the status of various Indian groups as federal wards. Although the Pueblos were not "terminated," they were affected by an accompanying federal relocation program that called for the removal of Indians from their homelands to one of six urban centers (Los Angeles, San Francisco–Oakland–San Jose, Denver, Dallas–Fort Worth, Chicago, and Cleveland) where presumably economic opportunity would be greater, thus speeding the Indians' assimilation into mainstream American society.

The Indian participants in the program were lured to the big cities by promises of wealth, but once there most were given insufficient training and inadequate support to assist them in the transition period. Many Indians were intentionally relocated to those cities that were farthest from their homes, making it difficult for them to return home. Extended family ties were greatly weakened. As the first chosen for the program were those deemed best equipped, by reason of education, intelligence, age, and social skills, to adapt to city life, the program constituted a kind of government-subsidized "brain drain" on the Indian communities. The promised jobs in the cities often did not materialize, and those that were available often paid low salaries. Urban poverty was now added to the list of woes besetting the nation's Native American population. In the big cities, Indians could not rely, to the same degree, on the communal ties that had always bound their communities, particularly as the program intentionally attempted to place Indians from the same tribe or community in different locations so as to force assimilation. Most Indians who took part in the urban relocation program moved back to their homelands after a short time, and the program was judged a failure.

Other termination programs also affected the Pueblo. One purpose of termination was to shift as many services as possible from the control of the Bureau of Indian Affairs to the appropriate federal departments. Some of the consequences for the Pueblos were that Indian children began attending public schools rather than special, specifically Indian institutions. Health services in the Pueblo community improved substantially beginning in 1955, when it was placed under the control of the U.S. Health Department, which had substantially more resources, in terms of funds and personnel, at its disposal than did the BIA.

The termination philosophy was reversed under the administrations of John F. Kennedy and Lyndon Johnson, who encouraged an increased federal presence, in terms of social programs, in Indian life. For the Pueblos, such programs meant new government funds for schools and various building projects. Tourism continued to grow in importance as a source of income for the Pueblos, who achieved an even greater renown for their skill as artists. Many Pueblos began attending art schools, where they learned modern techniques to go along with their traditional skills. Money from the sale of Pueblo crafts constituted an ever more important proportion of the Pueblo economy.

One of the most significant events in modern Pueblo history took place in 1970, when President Richard Nixon signed a bill deeding 48,000 acres of Carson National Forest in northern New Mexico, including Sacred Blue Lake, to Taos Pueblo. The Pueblos of Taos had been working for 64 years to regain legal control of this territory, which held great religious as well as economic significance for them.

For the last two decades, Pueblo life has been shaped by the same economic forces that have affected the rest of the United States. Greatly reduced federal spending has meant a significant reduction of social welfare programs and resulting economic and cultural hardship. As elsewhere in America, many

jobs were lost in the Pueblo country (at a time of rapid growth in the Pueblo population), resulting in a heightened rate of migration to the cities and a further fraying of the social fabric.

Hard times have forced the Pueblo leadership to take new measures to uphold the community's tradition of economic self-sufficiency. Many pueblos have opened bingo parlors, with the proceeds being used to fund education and social programs. In 1975 the All Indian Pueblo Council established the Indian Pueblo Cultural Center in Albuquerque. The center includes a museum, lecture hall, performance space, shop, and restaurant. The objectives of the center are to promote understanding of Pueblo culture and to provide "economic and cultural benefits to the entire community."

The changes in the Pueblo economy that have taken place over the last 100 years have resulted in corresponding changes in the Pueblo way of life. Tourism and wage labor have replaced subsistence agriculture as the primary means of livelihood for most Pueblos. As a result, Pueblo family life has been altered. Children no longer tend fields as part of their morning chores, working side by side with their elders. Although they return on feast days, many Pueblos have moved away from the homeland in order to find work. The structure of Pueblo homes has also changed. Many Pueblo homes now contain American furnishings and such modern conveniences as electricity and indoor plumbing. Some Pueblo homes contain television sets—purveyors of the ideol-

A Pueblo girl with her pet at Tesuque. One reason for optimism about the future of the Pueblos is their birth rate: the Pueblo population has increased dramatically in recent decades.

ogy of the dominant culture, from which children learn about superheroes instead of traditional folktales. Many Pueblos now live as nuclear families rather than extended family units. However, despite geographic dispersal and other forces working to weaken them, extended family ties generally remain quite strong. Other facets of traditional Pueblo culture endure as well; feast days, especially, remain important as an expression of family and community ties.

Throughout their long history, the Pueblos have used various methods to adapt to cultural change. This process is ongoing. The Pueblos continue to revitalize their culture through the conscious process of reinforcing those aspects that are most valued. By being selective about which elements to adopt, the Pueblos have been able to incorporate elements from Spanish, Mexican, or American culture into their own lives without shattering the essential integrity of their own culture. These methods of adaptation have allowed the Pueblos to maintain their value systems and control the rate and extent of change. The result is that modern Pueblos retain traditional values and close communal ties. No matter what the circumstances, the Pueblos have always been able to adapt to change while maintaining their identity as a people. This cultural tenacity has sustained them through the era of the conquistadores, the arrival of Spanish and then Mexican and American settlers, and the loss of much of their land, and it promises to sustain them through whatever challenges are to come in the 21st century. ▲

BIBLIOGRAPHY

Bancroft, Hubert Howe. *History of Arizona and New Mexico: 1530–1888.* San Francisco: The History Co., Publishers, 1889. Reprint. Albuquerque, NM: Horn and Wallace Press, 1962.

Benedict, Ruth. *Patterns of Culture.* New York: Penguin Books, 1947.

Bolton, Herbert Eugene, ed. *The Oñate Expeditions; Spanish Explorations; Spanish Exploration in the Southwest, 1542–1706.* New York: Scribners, 1908.

Bowden, Henry Warner. *American Indians and Christian Missions: Studies in Cultural Conflict.* Chicago and London: University of Chicago Press, 1981.

Collier, John. *From Every Zenith: A Memoir and Some Essays on Life and Thought.* Denver: Sage, 1963.

Dominguez, Francisco Atanasio. *The Missions of New Mexico, 1776.* Translated and annotated by Eleanor B. Adams and Fray Angelico Chavez. Albuquerque: University of New Mexico Press, 1956.

Dozier, Edward P. *The Pueblo Indians of North America.* New York: Holt, Rinehart & Winston, 1970.

Erdoes, Richard. *The Pueblo Indians.* New York: Funk & Wagnalls, 1967.

Espinosa, Jose Manuel. *The Pueblo Revolt of 1696 and the Franciscan Missionaries in New Mexico.* Norman: University of Oklahoma Press, 1988.

Hodge, Frederick W., and Theodore H. Lewis, eds. *The Coronado Narrative: Spanish Explorers in the Southern United States, 1528–1543.* New York: Scribners, 1970.

Horgan, Paul. *Great River: The Rio Grande in North American History.* Vol. 1, *The Indians and Spain.* New York: Holt, Rinehart & Winston, 1961.

Jones, Oakah L., Jr. *Pueblo Warriors and Spanish Conquest.* Norman: University of Oklahoma Press, 1966.

Ortiz, Alfonso, ed. *New Perspectives on the Pueblos.* Albuquerque: University of New Mexico Press, 1972.

Sando, Joe S. *Pueblo Nations: Eight Centuries of Pueblo Indian History.* Santa Fe: Clear Light Publishers, 1992.

Spicer, Edward H. *Cycles of Conquest.* Tucson: University of Arizona Press, 1967.

THE PUEBLO AT A GLANCE

TRIBE   *Pueblo*
CULTURE AREA   *Southwest*
GEOGRAPHY   *New Mexico and Arizona*
LINGUISTIC FAMILY   *Tanoan, Keresan, Zuni, Hopi*
CURRENT POPULATION   *55,000*
FIRST CONTACT   *Francisco de Coronado, Spanish, 1540*
FEDERAL STATUS   *Recognized*

GLOSSARY

adobe Building material made of sun-dried earth and straw.

aboriginal The first of its kind in a region.

agent A person appointed by the Bureau of Indian Affairs to supervise U.S. government programs on a reservation and/or in a specific region.

alcalde A chief of a Pueblo town; a position established by the Spanish but soon adapted by the Pueblos for their own uses.

All Indian Pueblo Council An organization of Pueblo leaders that existed originally to counteract nomadic raiding tribes around the years A.D. 1400 or A.D. 1525. The modern date of origin for this group is usually given as 1598, when Juan de Oñate met with 38 Indian leaders in the hope of colonizing Pueblo country.

anthropology The study of the physical, social, and historical characteristics of human beings.

archaeology The recovery and reconstruction of human ways of life through the study of material culture (including tools, clothing, and food and human remains).

artifact An object of historical interest produced by human workmanship.

assimilation The complete absorption of one group into another group's cultural tradition.

band A loosely organized group of people who are bound together by the need for food and defense, by family ties, and/or by other common interests.

breechcloth A strip of animal skin or cloth that is drawn between the legs and hung from a belt tied around the waist.

Bureau of Indian Affairs (BIA) A federal government agency now within the Department of the Interior. Originally intended to manage trade and other relations with Indians, the BIA now seeks to develop and implement programs that encourage Indians to manage their own affairs and to improve their educational opportunities and general social and economic well-being.

cacique A Pueblo chief.

compartmentalization The process of outwardly adopting ideas of another culture while not truly believing in them.

culture The learned behavior of humans; nonbiological, socially taught activities; the way of life of a group of people.

dialect A regional variant of a particular language with unique elements of grammar, pronunciation, and vocabulary.

encomiendas Land grants given to Spanish soldiers for five years of service. These grants were provided to encourage colonization.

entrada Spanish expeditions of exploration and conquest in the Americas; literally means entrance in Spanish.

fanega A Spanish unit of measurement.

Indian Reorganization Act (IRA) The 1934 federal law, sometimes known as the Wheeler-Howard Act, that ended the policy of allotting plots of land to individuals and encourged the development of reservation communities. The act also provided for the creation of autonomous tribal governments.

kivas (**also** *estufas*) Secret circular underground ceremonial chambers where Pueblos came together for religious worship.

mesa A flat-topped, tablelike hill.

mission A religious center founded by advocates of a particular denomination who are trying to convert nonbelievers to their faith.

missionaries Advocates of a particular religion who travel to convert nonbelievers to their faith.

munitions War matériel, especially guns and ammunition.

New Mexico Enabling Act of 1910 Legislation by which the Pueblos were legally brought under federal jurisdiction under terms similar to those of other Indian peoples.

paten A plate made of silver or gold used to carry the Eucharist in the Catholic mass.

Pueblo Lands Act A law passed in Congress in 1924 deeming that all non-Indian settlers prove continuous ownership of land. Monetary payment was given to the Pueblos for any land lost due to the failure of the United States to prosecute illegal settlers.

repartimiento The right of *encomienda* owners to employ Pueblo Indians living near the grants.

rescates Fairs where trading occurred.

reservation A tract of land retained by Indians for their own occupation and use.

tequitato A Pueblo leader who functions as a sheriff, carrying out the orders of the *cacique*.

termination Federal policy, in effect from the late 1940s through the 1960s, designed to cut costs by removing Indian tribes from government supervision and Indian lands from trust status.

territory A defined region of the United States that is not, but may become, a state. The government officials of a territory are appointed by the president, but territory residents elect their own legislature.

treaty A contract negotiated between representatives of the U.S. government and another sovereign nation, or nations, including Indian tribes. Treaties dealt with the cessation of military action, the surrender of political independence, the establishment of boundaries, terms of land sales, and related matters.

tribe A society consisting of several or many separate communities united by kinship, culture, language, and other social institutions, including clans, religious organizations, and warrior societies.

INDEX

PICTURE CREDITS

DR. ALFONSO ORTIZ is a professor of anthropology at the University of New Mexico, Albuquerque. Born in San Juan pueblo, he is the author of several publications, including *Tewa World: Space, Time and Becoming in a Pueblo Society* (1972), and editor of *New Perspectives on the Pueblos* (1985).

FRANK W. PORTER III, general editor of INDIANS OF NORTH AMERICA, is director of the Chelsea House Foundation for American Indian Studies. He holds a B.A., M.A., and Ph.D. from the University of Maryland. He has done extensive research concerning the Indians of Maryland and Delaware and is the author of numerous articles on their history, archaeology, geography, and ethnography. He was formerly director of the Maryland Commission on Indian Affairs and American Indian Research and Resource Institute, Gettysburg, Pennsylvania, and he has received grants from the Delaware Humanities Forum, the Maryland Committee for the Humanities, the Ford Foundation, and the National Endowment for the Humanities, among others. Dr. Porter is the author of *The Bureau of Indian Affairs* in the Chelsea House KNOW YOUR GOVERNMENT series.